The World According to
MANAGER MARK

The World According to
MANAGER MARK

MARK JENKINS

JOHN BLAKE

Published by John Blake Publishing Ltd,
3 Bramber Court, 2 Bramber Road,
London W14 9PB, England

www.johnblakebooks.com

www.facebook.com/johnblakebooks ⬛

twitter.com/jblakebooks ⬛

This edition published in 2015

ISBN: 978 1 78418 816 0

British Library Cataloguing-in-Publication Data:

A catalogue record for this book is available from the British Library.

Design by www.envydesign.co.uk

Printed in Great Britain by CPI Group (UK) Ltd

3 5 7 9 10 8 6 4 2

Illustrations by Andrew Pinder

Papers used by John Blake Publishing are natural, recyclable products made from
wood grown in sustainable forests. The manufacturing processes conform to the
environmental regulations of the country of origin.

Every attempt has been made to contact the relevant copyright-holders,
but some were unobtainable. We would be grateful if the appropriate
people could contact us.

To My Wonderful Mum, Stella
*Thank you for giving me something that money can't buy
and no one can ever take away from me… not even the bloody banks:
Your amazing sense of humour!!!*

Special thanks to
Andy Merriman
without whom this book wouldn't be half as good as it is!

Contents

Foreword

I believe it is customary to include a brief 'foreword', which apparently means 'word before'. Although obviously not just one word, so maybe it should be called 'forewords'. I guess if they put it at the back of the book, it would be called a 'backwords'!

Now I know traditionally someone else often writes this but I've never been a fan of what people tend to say about me so, to be on the safe side, I'm writing it myself.

Many of you will know me from Channel 4's award-winning comedy documentary series *The Hotel*. I was in three series; a grand total of twenty-five episodes. Two of the series featured The Grosvenor (pronounced 'GroveSnor') Hotel in Sunny Torquay and my exploits as the owner/manager until my eventual demise when I was forced to sell it (mainly due to the bloody banks and the global credit crunch, which definitely wasn't my fault, btw!) and the latest and third series featured the Cavendish Hotel, also in Sunny Torquay, and saw me undertake a temporary role for a summer season as the Entertainments Manager.

The Hotel was, for a time, one of Channel 4's most popular and talked-about TV programmes, attracting up to 2.8 million viewers, and was, in fact, shown in many other countries around the world as far away as New Zealand and even places like Holland, where they don't speak English so they had to add subtitles! (I still think it would have been better to dub it.)

The good news is that, even if you're one of the other sixty-one million or so people who live in this wonderful country of ours and have no idea what I'm talking about (to be fair, being shown at 8 pm on a Sunday night meant it clashed with *Antiques Roadshow, Call the Midwife* and even bloody *Top Gear*!) – if you've never even heard of *The Hotel*, let alone watched it – the good news is that this book isn't about the TV series.

So if you haven't already, you should definitely buy it!

Hooray!!!

Please Note

Any resemblance to any actual persons living or dead is entirely intentional as this book is factual and not, as you might expect, a work of fiction. All the stories and events contained within these pages are 100 per cent true and did really happen. Although some of the details may have changed, not to protect anyone or anything like that but because I have such a terrible bloody memory!!!

See www.officialmarkjenkins.com for even more hilarious material.

A

AGEING

I've never understood ageing. My lack of awareness is based on my occasionally extensive knowledge of history, which you might find hard to believe. You see, at one time, there was no such thing as AGEING! Prehistoric man never had a problem with it, as the average life expectancy back then was only between twenty-five to forty years, and even less for women. That seems strange, doesn't it? What with the hunter-gatherer men going out with their clubs to find food and the women back safely in their caves, nervously awaiting their return. Perhaps the caves were damp and the women caught chills and died, or maybe they died of boredom because they didn't have any daytime telly to watch!

And if you didn't die from the cold or weren't eaten by

dinosaurs, starvation got you, which wasn't a pleasant way to go. But the good thing about dying young during the Jurassic Age was that you still looked pretty good. You see, wrinkles hadn't been invented and, while some unlucky men went bald, for most of them the grey hairs were only just appearing!

I actually think I've aged quite well – I haven't developed a middle-aged paunch and I have a full head of hair. Did you know, at one stage, it was actually a toss-up between me and David Ginola for L'Oréal shampoo advertisements? In fact, the only way of telling my age is if you count the rings under my eyes. I'm lucky that I don't have to resort to artificial methods of maintaining my youthful looks. I don't think I ever will: cod-liver capsules aren't for me (I'm not a fan of fish or offal). Botox is out – you seem to end up looking perfectly frightened, a bit like a startled Cliff Richard – and although cosmetic surgery can hide a multitude of chins, as far as I'm concerned, the only results of a facelift are raised eyebrows.

The problem is that, for most people, once they start, they can't stop (a bit like watching darts or snooker), until in the end they barely resemble a normal human being. The biggest con ever has to be anti-ageing creams. They don't work! The problem is that, by the time you find out you need lotions or potions, it's too late. You can hardly go back to Boots twenty years after you started buying some expensive anti-ageing cream and demand a refund because the twenty-year-old receipt has fewer wrinkles and is in better condition than your face.

Some women are shy about their age – about ten years shy, I've found – and so the way I can tell a woman's true age is by the state of her elbows. No matter how much plastic surgery, Botox or make-up women slap on their face, the elbows never lie. It's true!

(Women everywhere are now rolling up their sleeves and inspecting their elbows!)

If ageing really bothers you, I suggest that the safest thing to do is stay indoors, make full use of dimmer switches and – most important of all – remove all the mirrors from your house.

And always remember that the alternative to ageing is far worse. I mean, which would you rather: end up with a face like Alan Sugar or be eaten by a bloody dinosaur?!?

ALCOHOL

It's no secret that I don't drink. Well, that's not quite true. I do have a tiny bit of alcohol sometimes but only very rarely. I have been known to have the odd tipple of Bacardi, providing it's completely drowned by copious amounts of lemonade so that the taste of the rum is hardly noticeable. You see, I'm a cheap date. Not only do I not eat much, I also hardly ever drink.

On even rarer occasions, the odd sip of champagne has passed my lips, although it has to be really good quality. Vintage, naturally. None of your sparkling-wine cheap rubbish. Or, as I like to call it, 'Nearly Champagne'. And because of this, I've never actually been what you would call drunk – well, not to the extent that I haven't known what I was doing… then again, half the time I don't really know what I'm doing anyway. But on the odd occasion I've had a little too much, my speech starts to slur a bit, I sound louder than usual and, like a chocolate soufflé, I wobble slightly. It's at this stage that I tend to switch to lemonade (no cheap stuff – it must be White's) or, better still, a nice latte.

The thing that really puzzles me is 'alcohol-free' drinks with alcoholic names: alcohol-free lager, beer and even wine. And alcohol-free wine isn't wine – it's bloody grape juice (see W for WINE).

Soon they'll start manufacturing alcohol-free alcohol. I hardly ever drink alcohol not just because I don't want to get drunk – I simply don't like the taste of it. So why anyone would want to pretend they are drinking an alcoholic drink when it really isn't one is quite beyond me.

THE WORLD ACCORDING TO MANAGER MARK

Did you know that one famous teetotaller was astronaut Buzz Aldrin? He was the second man to walk on the moon – you see, he didn't need alcohol to get high!

B

BICYCLES

Without wishing to sound like Jeremy Clarkson, I'm not a lover of bikes on the road. In fact, to be honest, as a car driver, they are a bloody nuisance and very dangerous. They don't half make a mess of your car if you're unfortunate enough to collide with one of them!

When I was younger and at school, I did actually ride a bike... although we weren't allowed to ride a bicycle to school unless we had passed our Cycling Proficiency Test, which basically involved being able to ride it around a load of strategically placed roadwork cones. I guess, with hindsight, it was good practice for when we actually got to ride on the real roads!

But not only are cyclists now allowed on the road without any type of test but they also seem to think that the basic rules don't apply to them. I know that nowadays cycling is considered the Green thing to do but, as you will see from the content of the book, I'm not a lover of anything green. What really are a nonsense are these politicians who think, if they are seen to cycle everywhere, it will make them appear more ecologically correct and, therefore, more popular. Of course, when you find out that all their laptops, umbrellas, briefcases and sandwiches are actually being carried in a big petrol-guzzling limo just behind them, it seems rather hypocritical.

I think cyclists should actually be banned from using roads and, although this might sound a tad autocratic, it's actually for their benefit. I'm thinking of them! You see, I really don't think the roads are a safe place for cyclists – they're much too dangerous, especially with these huge juggernauts and supermarket delivery lorries hogging the roads (now, there's an idea – maybe we should ban all of those too!)

One of the most bizarre sights is cyclists trying to peddle up a steep hill, wobbling about all over the place. It doesn't matter how many gears they have, they still struggle and gradually become slower and slower, until pedestrians are actually over-taking them. Do they get off and push it up the hill, which would be, by far, the easier and faster option? No, this is seen as some kind of failure and yet, when they approach traffic lights, they are more than happy to hop off and push their bicycle through the red lights! For me, bicycles should stay where they belong… in the safe and secure environment of the gym!

BOOKS

There's a chap called Kanye West – I think he is some kind of polar explorer – who once said he was a proud non-reader of books. I have to agree with him. I'm not sure what there is to be learned from reading books (although some instructional manuals can be useful, particularly if there's a puncture in your inflatable). No, I'm one of the few people who can claim they've written more books than they've actually read. Well… one more, to be precise. This one! Between us, I'm not really a reader and could never be described as a bookworm.

Of course, this particular book is different and should be read by everyone, as not only is it extremely interesting, hilarious and educative (see my reference to Kanye West on the first line), it will bring me in some meagre earnings – unless, of course, you borrow it from a library, when I will earn precisely 2.2 pence every time it's borrowed. Well that's not going to get my Bentley back! And I hope that this is your own copy and you haven't borrowed it from a friend because then I won't even receive the 2.2 pence.

Talking of libraries, I've only ever been to one once and that was to pin up a notice about a support group for ex-hoteliers. I didn't like the place because it was full of books, which somewhat disturbed me, and, when I asked a librarian – a middle-aged woman in a tweed skirt and wearing a monocle – for a drawing pin, she had the cheek to 'shush' me. Unbelievable! And me, with my *sotto voce* voice (that's Latin for 'mumbling'). I immediately took against librarians – harridans all – and libraries in general and made a solemn oath never to darken their doors again. Now, I understand, they are more like playgroups, with lots of children's activities and readings. There must be an awful lot of 'shushing' these days.

You know, since someone invented television (hang on... maybe *that* was Kanye West) I don't see the point in bothering to print any books. There's so much to watch on telly. I mean, you can't spend an evening staring at a whole pile of books in the corner of your living room, can you? And when you get bored with one book, you have to get up to change the title; there isn't a remote where you can flip to another book until you find something you eventually like – which you can do with the good old telly. Apparently, there is an electronic device called a Kindle, which you can load books onto. I always thought kindle was something you used to start fires with but then again, I suppose you can also light fires using books.

In actual fact, to be honest, I am actually glad there are such things as books, otherwise I'd be sat at home with nothing to do instead of writing this one. My problem is I've always thought people who have loads of books to be complete show-offs. It's not that they have them; it's the fact that they have this desire to show them off as a way of impressing all their friends and appearing intellectual. They're saying, 'Look at me! I've read all these books and have all this knowledge now stored in my brain... and so I'm far superior to you.'

Well, I suppose with all that knowledge, they probably are but they don't need to rub my nose in it. Perhaps they are all frustrated librarians. Of course, this book is different: this one should take pride of place on your bookshelf and you should show it off to everyone!

But if you have to read a book, I do have one helpful tip: always choose something that will make you look good if you're suddenly taken ill – especially if you don't pull through. I suggest this book as an excellent example. And then, as the paramedics are loading you onto a stretcher and covering your head in a blanket, they'll say, 'What a shame about poor old [INSERT NAME HERE] but at least they went out reading something life-affirming and self-improving.'

Maybe books do have their place as long as it's not mine! But I'll finish with a quote to show you how literary I could be if I really bothered: 'Outside of a dog, a book is a man's best friend. Inside of a dog it's too dark to read.'

That's by Groucho Marx, who I think was some sort of Communist.

BRITISH PUBLIC

Or the 'Great Unwashed', to give them their proper name.

People often ask me what it's like suddenly becoming famous and having the Great British Public know who you are. The truth is that sometimes it's a bit of a nightmare, mainly because of my terrible memory. I have such a bad memory that, whereas most people walk into a room and forget what they came in for, I even forget to walk into the room! I'm not very good with faces and often forget names. They say that memories are made of this – whatever this is. I wouldn't know. Crikey! You see what I mean? I've actually forgotten what topic I'm meant to be writing about. I could never be a policeman: I'd never recognise those faces on the wanted posters. I'd let all the criminals just walk past me.

Anyway, where was I? Oh yes...

There was an outcry a few years ago when it was suggested that everyone should carry an identity card. Well, if I had my way, we'd go a step further and, every time we went out, we would all have to wear a big name badge so at least we'd all know who everyone was!

I feel I should know members of the public when they approach me and it can be a bit awkward. Sometimes I'm walking along the street and someone will come over, greet me like a long-lost friend and start a conversation with me as if they have known me all their life. I have no idea who they are and I go into panic mode. They'll ask me about my dear old mum and all sorts and I'm desperately trying to remember who they are, but can't for the life of me recall where I would have met them. Then it will dawn on me – they've obviously seen me on the telly!

Don't get me wrong: I love meeting and talking to people but what they don't understand is that TV sets aren't a two-way mirror. Just because they've seen me doesn't mean I've seen them! I have no idea who they are. If they started the conversation with, 'Hello, you don't know me but I've seen you on television,' I'd be fine. So the thing is, if any of you reading this do bump into me on the street, I suggest that be your introductory line and then I'll be prepared.

The worst thing has to be when I'm out shopping and I get recognised. I notice that, as they are engaging me in conversation, people look in my basket and crane their necks to see what I've bought. Perhaps they know I have an eye for a bargain, although it can't be of any help when we're in Poundland. In fact, I'm now so paranoid that I tend to hide certain things in the bottom of my basket, just in case that happens. That did lead to an unfortunate incident at the checkout when the girl on the till thought I was trying to smuggle a lamb chop under my copy of *Trainspotters Weekly* without paying. I soon put her right. A free autograph and a selfie can often save the day.

BUS LANES

Now, I'm not really one for public transport and, if I'm honest, the last time I actually travelled on a bus was way back in 1977. Might even have been a charabanc. In fact, my main incentive for passing my driving test when I was seventeen and as soon as I could was so that I no longer had to travel on buses.

BUS LANES

When I was at school, I'd get a bus most days and back then they used to have a conductor collecting the fares as well as a driver to drive the bus. My favourite trick was making sure that, as it approached my stop, I was the first passenger off the bus and, if the conductor was distracted, I'd reach up and ring the bell twice – the signal to the driver that everyone was off and he could drive on.

I was very amused watching the other kids being driven on to the next stop, knowing they'd have to walk all the way back. That was until one day when the driver was looking in his mirror and saw me ring the bell and reported me to the school! I got into a lot of trouble and since then I've never really been a fan of buses. In fact, I've always considered them for people too lazy to pass a driving test or too poor to own a car!

Nowadays buses are considered ecologically correct and the Green way to travel. As such, they are given priority on the roads to encourage more people to use public transport and so bus lanes have been created! As a car driver, a bus lane can be a bloody nightmare, especially in cities. One minute it's there and the next it's disappeared or it's moved. You find yourself dodging them so that it feels like you're playing some sort of 'Traffic Hopscotch'.

Apparently, the idea is that in heavy traffic, if buses have their own lane, it means that they won't be delayed and they'll become more efficient and arrive on time. In that way, more people will be encouraged to use them. To make sure normal people like car drivers don't clog up bus lanes, cars are subject to a fine if they drive in them. Of course, most cities only have this rule at certain times of the day and these regulations are relaxed when the roads are empty to save you having to weave in and out dodging them. Blimey… I could work for Transport for London with that kind of detailed knowledge of the philosophy of bus lanes. I think I'll have a word with Boris, or whoever the Mayor of London is, in due course.

Last Christmas we decided to have a nice family Yuletide dinner with my dear old mum in Sunny Torquay. My son, Harry, lives in Plymouth so I arranged to drive the 30 miles to go and pick him up. I know the town quite well as I actually lived there for a while. Once Harry was in the car, we headed back to Torquay, enjoying the freedom of the open road and lack of traffic (this was about 10 am on Christmas Day). As I was leaving Plymouth it appeared that they'd changed the routes around the town and, instead of taking a direct, straight course, there were signs taking us a long way round.

I wasn't really paying attention because I knew where I was, but I suddenly found myself confronted by a bus lane. In fact, what used to be the whole road and the main way out of Plymouth was now a much-despised bus lane. Harry warned me and pointed it out. I told him not to worry and smiled paternally: 'It's Christmas day – there aren't any buses out today.' I drove on through the deserted roads and reached Torquay in plenty of time for a wonderful Christmas lunch, after which I took Harry home.

Two weeks later I received a letter from Plymouth City Council, which enclosed a photograph of my car driving along an absolutely deserted road – all you could see were the words

'Bus Lane' clearly written in the middle of the road. They'd fined me £60... SIXTY POUNDS!

The whole fine system is there to ensure that you don't drive in bus lanes and hold up buses. But it was Christmas Day... I wasn't holding up any buses. Because on Christmas Day there weren't any bloody buses!!!

Happy Bloody Christmas. Unbelievable!

C

CAFÉS

I've been a coffee drinker as long as I can remember – in fact, long before anyone in this country had even heard of a double-shot espresso or a single-shot latte, let alone the numerous cafés, outlets and coffee-shop chains. And I've always had my coffee made with all milk – not soya, skimmed, lactose-free, condensed or organic, but full-fat cow!

Now, when you're a smoker, having a coffee is like a trigger to light up. In fact, when I once gave up smoking for six weeks, the only way I could do it successfully was to give up drinking coffee and hot chocolate at the same time. But it was a disastrous decision – I just couldn't cope without my nicotine, caffeine and Ovaltine and it resulted in me becoming miserable. In fact, I became so depressed that I had to start smoking again.

I thought I'd rather be happy, taking all the health risks associated with smoking and coffee, than be miserable and live a longer life. Even if I didn't live any longer, life without cigarettes and the odd latte would certainly feel a bloody sight longer!

I like frequenting cafés but, since the smoking ban, the few tables outside on the pavement where you can actually smoke have become like gold dust to us smokers. Especially we single people. One of the worst things about being single (OK, not the worst – that's the single supplement on hotel rooms, which I would never implement unless coerced by outside market forces) is that, when you go out for a coffee and you're alone, you can end up walking past several coffee shops until you finally spot an empty outside table. You dash inside to order your latte only to find that, by the time you've been served, someone else has taken it and you're stood outside holding your coffee with nowhere to sit – unless you go back inside, of course, but then you can't have a cigarette.

I wouldn't mind but half the time the bloody tables are taken up with non-smokers. I think it only fair that, if you are a non-smoker and you happen to be sat outside, you give up your seat to us smokers. The smoking ban has worked – you have, after all, got your own way. Either that or all the tables outside coffee shops should be reserved for Smokers Only!

So, if you want to enjoy some fresh air with your coffee, it's simple… all you'll have to do is start smoking!

And, of course, ordering your drink of choice has now become the most convoluted process since they invented the

Eurovision Song Contest voting system. I used to be quite happy with teaspoon of Gold Blend in warm milk but that's nowhere to be found. You can't even order a simple black or a white coffee now. Oh no! A coffee with milk is a 'Long Flat White' and a black coffee is an 'Americano'.

And then there are the various sizes to contend with: the 'Tall' can apparently be short, but is the 'Skinny' less tall than the 'Regular' or not? The Grande isn't as big as the Venti but the Venti is smaller than the Trenta (which sounds like twenty but means thirty in Italian, which is fine if you live in Italy). I have no idea how the Primo compares to the Medio or the Massimo, which I always thought was a mountain range in Chile.

While I was queuing up in a branch of a well-known coffee outlet, I'm sure I once heard someone order a double de-clutched triple-roasted Hibiscus Chai macchiato (shaken not stirred) with no foam but a three-pump peppermint whip. And the assistant simply smiled philosophically and asked for the customer's name, which, somewhat surprisingly, turned out to be Bert…

It's all so complicated – it's no wonder that the staff who make the coffee are all fully qualified barristers.

CARS

If you're visiting an expensive car showroom and have to pose the famous question, 'How many miles to the gallon does this do?' then you obviously can't afford the car. The reality is that, when you buy a really expensive motor, the true cost isn't how much petrol it uses but how much money you lose when you sell it.

I paid £115,000 for my original Bentley (it was so opulent it didn't purr – it sneered) and after six years all I got when I sold it was £30,000! The depreciation was £300 a week!

When I realised how much it really cost to own a Bentley, I was too scared to drive it! I certainly couldn't afford to pay for petrol as well. It would have been cheaper just to take bloody taxis everywhere.

Talking of mpg, why do car manufactures still only quote how many miles to a gallon a car can do when you haven't been able to buy petrol by the gallon for as long as I can remember? And why do pubs still sell beer in pints but wine and spirits in millilitres? Then again, I never understood what a gill was when the measure was 1/6 of a gill and not 25 ml. What's a millilitre anyway? I don't suppose anyone knows. That's something they don't teach in schools. And they certainly never mention gills!

Sorry, I'm meant to be talking about cars.

I've owned quite a few different cars over the years and it has to be said, despite my love of Bentleys and other luxury motors, one of the favourite cars I've ever owned was also one of the cheapest – an old Hillman Imp, which cost me £120! One day the engine blew up and I managed to get a second-hand engine supplied and fitted for just £60!

Now, for my young readership, a Hillman Imp was a tiny two-door hatchback. Well, when I say hatchback, the engine was in the boot and the rear windscreen actually opened to reveal a sort of small boot space/parcel shelf above the engine where you could put your shopping. This wasn't ideal if you got stuck in traffic on the way home and you had a tub of ice cream heating up, although it was perfect if you'd nipped out for fish and chips, which were still warm when you got home!

The engine being in the boot made the car unique because you didn't have a lumpy bit going from the gear stick to the engine in the front, so the front footwell was flat and, because it was such a small, narrow car, there wasn't a lot of space between the passenger and driver.

So my favourite trick if I was out driving alone was to slide along onto the passenger seat where I could still just about reach the pedals! I'd steer by holding the bottom of the wheel with one hand while hidden from view. Driving along, I'd hang my other arm out of the window, waving and pointing and giving the appearance that I was just a passenger… and that no one was actually driving the car!

I'd sometimes amuse myself by driving around roundabouts several times and getting bemused looks from pedestrians and other drivers who couldn't understand who was driving or what was going on. You see, you don't need a satnav to drive around in circles!

Of course, you couldn't do that nowadays because small cars, such as the Mini or Fiat 500, now have giant versions. The latest Mini Clubman 5-Door Estate is about the same size as some people carriers, although they still call it a Mini! And the Fiat 500 was so named because that was the size of the engine. The car had a tiny 500cc one and now that they've produced a giant version… and it's still called a 500! I know there are worse things in the world but, to my mind, they shouldn't be allowed to do that.

Anyway, after I sold my Bentley, I bought an old banger. In fact, it's so old that it's insured for fire, damage, theft and Zeppelin raids.

I do have one tip though, now that we no longer need to display our Tax Disc: instead of throwing away a perfectly good holder and being left with a sticky windscreen, why not use it to display a picture of your favourite person or a loved one? You could also always do what I've done and find a suitable photo to scare off would-be car thieves. I suggest an image of Jeremy Clarkson.

CHILDBIRTH

I think this whole childbirth thing has got out of hand and especially after-birth – although that can mean something else entirely and is not to be read about over breakfast, or any meal for that matter. No, I'm referring to post-childbirth. Nowadays, not only do the women get a whole year off work to get over having a baby but even the men can take two weeks off as 'paternity leave'. Paternity leave?! What on earth is that supposed to be? It never existed when my children were born. Years ago in China they never made such a fuss. Most of the time the women gave birth in their lunch breaks and then carried on working the afternoon shifts in the rice fields! And no one was any the worse off, became angry or got into a paddy – well except for the pregnant women rice pickers.

I actually didn't take any time off work and was present at one of my children's births, although I nearly missed it!

Towards the end of her third pregnancy, my wife went into labour one night and so, thinking the baby was about to arrive, we rushed to the hospital, only to be told by the midwife that it was a false alarm and that the baby definitely wouldn't arrive that night. As a precaution, however, the medical staff decided to keep my wife in hospital and, as it was getting late, the doctor told me I might as well go home and get a good night's sleep. Naturally, I thought that was a great idea, knowing that it was probably going to be the last time I'd get a decent kip for a while!

So I went home, took to my bed and was fast asleep when I was woken at 3 am by the telephone ringing. It was the hospital.

Could I get there as quickly as possible as the baby was on its way… NOW!!!

I was so excited, my heart skipped a beat; this was the one call I'd always dreamed of; something I'd always wanted. At long last, the experience of a lifetime! I jumped into the car knowing that this was my one and only opportunity… Yes, this was it! Finally, I could drive as fast as I liked, breaking all the speed limits and even go through all the red lights! I had the perfect excuse – because, if the police pulled me in, I'd tell them my wife was about to give birth and they'd not only let me off but they'd probably give me a police escort to the hospital!

So I arrived at the hospital in plenty of time and walked into the delivery room. My wife seemed to be moaning and groaning an awful lot. Making quite a fuss if you want to know. I wanted to tell her how exciting the drive had been but she didn't seem interested. I wouldn't have minded her being so preoccupied but she had already had a child – it wasn't as if it was the first time. She must have known what to expect!

However, for me it was different – this was my first time being present at a birth and so, naturally, I felt a bit uncomfortable and didn't really know what to do or expect. Well, I did… I knew she was expecting a baby. But what a palaver! I started to feel like I should be somewhere else, in between all the shouting and screaming and sucking on the gas and air. It was all very awkward. Then she suddenly looked over at me and noticed I was stood with my arms folded, staring out of the window, admiring my parking spot.

'What do you think you are doing?' she screamed.

'Nothing,' I replied innocently. 'I didn't think I had to do anything. After all, I did my bit nine months ago.' And with a disarming smile, I added, 'I thought it was your turn now!'

For some reason, it was at this point that she started to get really angry and just wouldn't stop shouting at me. Bit unfair, I thought, as I hadn't done anything to upset her. No, it was definitely all to do with her. But I didn't want to get cross with her because I assumed it was something to do with her hormones or something. Apparently, being pregnant and giving birth does strange things to you!

That was a night to remember and one of the most exciting of my life. What an experience! A dream come true. I couldn't believe it had finally happened to me. Yes... speeding through Torquay, going as fast as I wanted and ignoring all those red lights was something I'll never forget!

CHRISTMAS

I've never known why they always have the shortest day of the year just a few days before Christmas. It's daft. You'd have thought that, with so much to do getting ready for Christmas, what most people need are longer days just before, not bloody shorter ones!

I'm a bit more solvent now and not one of those poor people that I sometimes refer to – but before you start sending me begging letters, I'm not rich. There was a time when I had to budget very carefully and watch the pennies. And for those of you in a similar position, here are some money-saving (all right, penny-pinching) ideas for Christmas presents:

- Recycle old cards sent to you – just change the names.
- Instead of cooking turkey, why not use roadkill?
- Steal wreaths from funeral parlours for your front door.
- Buy 'past-their-sell-by-date' boxes of Milk Tray from Sainsbury's. One thing I've learned over the years is that EVERYONE LOVES MILK TRAY!!!
- Use newspapers as wrapping paper – but not *Sunday Sport*, which would be in very bad taste.
- Use grape juice instead of wine – most people can't tell the difference.
- Buy out-of-date advent calendars and change all the dates (time-consuming but very satisfying).
- Replace your Christmas tree with a lamp stand. With some holly and tinsel you can pass it off as some sort of pagan symbol.

I used to adore Christmas, although that was before I went into the hotel business when I had to work all over the holidays. But before then it was a special time with the family and, of course, what made it even more brilliant was the old adage that 'Christmas comes but once a year', which meant it was something to really look forward to. One of the highlights was the traditional Christmas Dinner, although it is something that I've never quite understood as, in reality, nobody really likes turkey that much. If we did find it that delicious, we'd eat it more than once a year!

Of course, everything changed when I bought my first hotel.

Then the festive season began in June when the Christmas-cracker salesman would call! In fact, most of the Christmas stuff had to be ordered in the summer because we catered mainly for coach parties off-season – so it meant Christmas actually started in mid-October!

Quite why coachloads of pensioners wanted to travel all the way to Torquay in October to celebrate 'a pretend Christmas' was beyond me, although I realise it was much cheaper for them than going away in December. So, for me, the 'Turkey & Tinsel' season actually arrived every autumn.

The entire hotel was decorated to look like Santa's grotto and the *Best Ever Christmas Carols* CD was played constantly on a loop, so not only did I learn the lyrics to every carol ever sung but I also discovered that 'A Virgin Unspotted' was actually a Christmas hymn.

As the holidaymakers arrived twice a week, it also meant that we had to celebrate Christmas twice a week. Every Tuesday and Saturday was Christmas Day, complete with turkey and Christmas pudding and, of course, a visit from Santa. And guess who played Father Christmas? Yes, you're right... Twice a week I'd stick a cushion up my jumper and don my Santa suit and hand out presents for everyone while wishing them all a very Merry Christmas! Ho, Ho, Bloody Ho!

The first year was a bit of a novelty but, after ten years in the business and having celebrating over 220 Christmases during that time, I have to be honest, the holiday started to lose its appeal. My yuletide feelings of goodwill turned to ill will. The worst bit was 'Twixmas' – the time between the actual

Christmas Day and before the New Year guests arrived when I had to do it all over again. There was a hotel in Torquay that used to run 'Turkey & Tinsel' right into March… almost six months of the year. If I'm honest, I'd have rather closed down – then there really would have been no room at the inn!!

COMPLAINTS

My pet hate is people who complain. Not that people shouldn't complain. They must and they should complain and never suffer in silence or – worse – moan about things and not do anything about it. In fact, I'm the biggest complainer of them all. I like to complain even if I haven't really got anything to complain about! No, what I can't stand are the customers who grumble when it's too late to do anything about their gripe – or, indeed, sometimes several gripes.

When I was in the hotel business, that was the one thing that really wound me up. Guests would stay the whole week, never say a bloody word, then the minute they got home they would either write a ten-page letter, listing every complaint known to man or – even more disastrously – go on the Internet and tell the whole world how rubbish they thought everything was. It could be the noisy occupants next door, the décor or the lack of room service. But it was often the beds: the size of the beds, location of the beds, the fact that they weren't four-posters, the fact that they *were* four-posters, the bedding on the beds, that the beds were too camp, too butch, too hard or too soft.

But did they once mention anything at the time? Oh no! Cowards, the lot of them. If they had mentioned something at the time, I'd have had a fighting chance of at least trying to put it right. But once they had left the premises, what could I do about it? I never understood why on earth, if you were that unhappy, you would keep quiet until it was too late to put anything right.

I used to treat all my guests exactly the same way, whatever I thought of them – especially when it came to complaints. I remember one couple arriving late and so, rather than going to their room, they went straight down to the dining room where all the other guests were having dinner. About five minutes later they reappeared at reception, stating that they were not going to stay in the hotel and demanding a full refund.

'What's wrong?' I asked.

'The food's rubbish,' the man said.

'What do you mean, rubbish? You'll have to be more specific.'

Now the woman chipped in. 'Just like he said. The food's rubbish. So we're not staying and we want a full refund.'

Now, while I accept that some of the dishes we served were a little dated, the food itself wasn't past its sell-by date! My chef was actually quite good and his best dishes were shepherd's pie and sticky toffee pudding – although you couldn't always tell which one you were eating. He certainly didn't go in for this modern fancy food. In fact, his idea of nouvelle cuisine was to put a sprig of parsley on the gammon and pineapple.

Anyway, back to my difficult couple. By this time I was more than somewhat annoyed.

'I'll tell you what,' I responded. 'I believe in treating everyone equally, so let's go down to the dining room. There are ninety-three guests currently eating their dinner and we'll ask each and every one if they think the food is "rubbish". If they agree with you, I'll give EVERYONE – not just you two – their money back. If the diners are happy with their food, well, it's obviously you two who are wrong and it's not the food we serve!'

They clearly weren't gamblers, refused to call my quadruple bluff (I think that's right), declined to take me up on my offer and so left without a refund.

I used to get all my guests, on arrival, to pay in full, just in case they forgot to pay on departure or somehow went broke during their stay! (As those of you who have holidayed in the West Country will know, the temptations for spending money in Torquay are many and wondrous.)

CONGESTION CHARGE

The biggest con ever (apart from anti-ageing cream: see 'A' for AGEING) has to be London's Congestion Charge.

I can sort of understand some bridges having a toll if they cost a fortune to build and they're going to save you an hour's extra driving. That's fair enough. I can just about put up with paying £2 for the privilege. But the Congestion Charge is something else.

Just after it was introduced some years ago, I had to travel up to London. I was quite a Rich Person back then: this was BD and BCC (Before Divorces and Before Credit Crunch!) and Rolls-Royce had invited me up to the unveiling of their new model. So I booked a suite at the hotel opposite, which had all my basic requirements – a four-poster bed, sunken bath and also a smoking suite, so I could have a cigarette with my coffee following breakfast in my own private sitting room. And, of course, valet parking. I would never stay in a hotel if I had to worry about where I was going to park the Bentley. I had heard about this Congestion Charge thing and I noticed an odd sign but I didn't see any barriers or anyone collecting money, as I was more concerned about following my satnav directions and not getting lost.

In any case, I had no intention of adding to the coffers of the local council by paying any kind of toll to enter the West End – after all, I was only there for one night and was going to leave my car at the hotel for my entire stay, so I wasn't even going to be driving around London. No, they weren't going to get any Congestion Charge out of me. Anyway, I arrived safely and was met by a porter who took my overnight bag out of the boot and then went to park the Bentley for me.

The following morning, when it was time to leave, the car was brought round and I set off back to Sunny Torquay. Oh, by the way, I didn't buy the new Rolls as it was far too big for me; I'd have needed a cushion to see over the steering wheel and long-vision glasses just to detect the end of the bonnet! I realised that I'd have never been able to park it in the crowded Sainsbury's car park without a periscope.

Two weeks later I was horrified to receive not one but TWO letters, both advising that I had been fined £80 – a total of £160 – for failing to pay the bloody Congestion Charge. Apparently, my hotel was just inside the zone, so they fined me for driving in and then again the following morning when I drove out. Unbelievable!

They could at least have a barrier and a man sat in a booth collecting the tenners in cash as you go in and out, not just leave you to notice an odd sign and then – without warning – make you pay £160!

I wouldn't mind but how can they justify charging anything? The bloody roads in central London aren't new – they've always been there! And they're still bloody congested!

If they built some sort of underground road system a bit like the Tube, in which you could nip round London in half the time while still in your car, I'd be happy to pay £10 but, until they do, I shall never drive into central London again.

D

DAFT LAWS

You may think that there are some daft laws in the United Kingdom that have exceeded their 'sell-by' date. But the thing is, much of the strangest legislation has never been repealed and so we unknowingly continue to live under its jurisdiction. Here are a few laws that you should be warned about… just in case.

- According to ancient statute, it is perfectly legal to murder a Scotsman within the ancient city walls of York but only if he is carrying a bow and arrow at the time. I bet not many Scotsmen living in York dare join the local archery club! Apparently, for some reason, this doesn't apply on a Sunday.
- Although, if it is a Sunday, it's not a great idea for any Welshmen to visit Hereford, where it's legal to shoot the

Welsh all day, provided the killing takes place with longbows, of course!

- And, apparently, MPs are not allowed into the House of Commons wearing armour, which is a pity because, with all the backstabbing that goes on in that place, quite a few politicians would find that sort of protection quite useful.

- MPs are also not allowed to die in the House of Commons. I can only assume they introduced that edict because of the worry that, if some of them did drop dead, you'd be hard pressed to tell!

- It is also illegal to eat mince pies anywhere in England on Christmas Day. Oliver Cromwell considered pies a forbidden pagan pleasure and on 22 December 1657 his Puritan Council banned consumption of mince pies on 25 December. (Obviously, when he was a boy, Santa must have forgotten him one year!)

- Not only is it illegal to hail a black cab in London – apparently, they can only accept fares if they are stationary – but the drivers are also required by law to ask if you have the plague. It is also mandatory for the cabbies to carry a bale of straw in the boot of their vehicle at all times. I suppose then you must hail them by shouting, 'HAY!'

And, believe it or not, I think one of the daftest recent laws relates to the smoking ban… the fact that it is still perfectly legal to be able to smoke in a hotel bedroom (providing it's been designated a smoking room). This coupled with the fact that hotel 'residents' can also purchase alcoholic drinks twenty-four hours a day to be consumed in their room if they wish.

So, if you have a hotel, it is technically legal to operate a sort of pub where you can not only serve drinks twenty-four hours a day regardless of local licensing laws but you can also allow your patrons to smoke inside while drinking! And all this without fear of the smoking police slapping an £80 fine on the guests! If all the designated smoking bedrooms have connecting doors, you can mingle with your friends and even have a game of dominos at any time of the day or night while enjoying a pint and a fag! And if it all becomes a bit much for you, you can even have a quick nap!

It's simple really to become a hotel 'resident'. All you have to do is sign a register on the way in, pay a token amount – say £1 – and collect a key. (In fact, I've stayed in a few where £1 would be overcharging!)

Sorry! I apologise… I seem to have strayed into 'H' for HOTELS when really I should be telling you about more daft laws. I'll check out now, but not without first informing you about some of the loony legislation from around the world – you see, it's not just the UK that is home to some ridiculous rules. It's a global phenomenon:

- In Canada it is absolutely forbidden to drag a dead horse along Toronto's streets before midday.
- In France it is illegal to name a pig 'Napoleon' or marry a dead person.
- In Thailand it's prohibited to leave your house without

wearing underwear (I have no idea how they check that out!).

• In Israel it's illegal to pick your nose on the Sabbath.

• In China the law states that a man mustn't eat another man's wife… intentionally.

• Bingo games cannot last more than five hours in North Carolina. (They must have been to one of my Party Nights!)

And here's one of my very own: if you're caught on a speed camera 5 mph over the limit while driving to Torquay, holding a cigarette out of your window and dressed as a penguin, you are sentenced to be Mark Jenkins for the rest of your life. Just think of that. Blimey!!!

DATING

The worst thing about being single is the whole business of dating, especially when you get to a certain age. It's different when you're younger because then your hormones make all the decisions, so you don't even have to think about it. It was quite simple: you either fancied someone or you didn't. In fact, half the time, even if you didn't really fancy someone, you'd end up going on a date with them, hoping that by the end of the night you'd change your mind!

I'm not much of an expert on dating, as I'm not that experienced, although I have to say I actually have a 100 per cent success rate. You see, I've been on two dates and both of them ended in marriage! (The trouble is that the marriages were also 100 per cent unsuccessful.)

But I do think that the older I get, the more fussy I have become and all this Internet-dating malarkey has made things ten times worse. Now you are encouraged to fill out pages and pages of information, stating exactly what you are looking for and including very personal details about yourself, such as the name of your favourite inflatable (DEREK), pastime (SMOKING) and vol-au-vent filling (MUST CONTAIN SOME KIND OF CHIPOLATA). In fact, whoever invented Internet dating should either be shot or told to do it themselves. The agencies are usually full of bloody nutcases and half the time you'd actually be safer and happier just spending the evening with your computer.

When I was younger, the girl with the biggest boobs was usually the most popular choice among boys in my class and the buxom types were usually claimed by the ones that got into the most trouble – the naughty kids. These girls were never interested in what your future prospects might be and they certainly weren't interested in what hobbies or interests you had.

Now every tiny detail of your life is examined and we're all encouraged to try to find the perfect partner, who they tell you will be your soulmate. That's where the problems begin because the female who you think of as 'The Perfect Partner' can often turn out to be the worst possible choice... well, that's how it's been for me!

Maybe I should just revert to my adolescent self, stick to the original plan and just find the woman with the biggest boobs!

DIET FOODS

To achieve best results, it will be to your advantage if you read this in conjunction with the FAT PEOPLE section, although be sure that you don't miss any of the topics in between because then you'll be at a disadvantage when this book becomes the subject of your book group. (That's especially for my north-London fans).

I've come to the conclusion that most Diet Foods rate among the biggest cons (along with the Congestion Charge and anti-wrinkle cream). If you're fatter than you want to be because you haven't followed my 'don't buy bigger clothes' plan (see 'F' for FAT PEOPLE), you may find yourself tempted to buy some of those special Diet Foods as a way of losing weight. In fact, some people will decide to start a diet and think the answer is to dash down to their local supermarket and fill up their trolley with everything that claims to be Diet Food because it contains fewer calories.

In that way, they believe they can eat the same foods as they were eating before but that, by some miracle, because it says Diet Food, they'll instantly lose weight. I can assure you, in most cases this simply doesn't work. Dieting is all about willpower and basic maths. If you consume more calories than you use, you'll get fat; on the other hand, if you consume less calories than you use, you'll lose weight and get thin. Simple really.

Of course, the actual amount of calories depends on which foods you eat and, more importantly, how many and how much. You see, this is where the problem lies with so-called special Diet Foods. While in the supermarket the other day, I noticed 'Special Slimmer's Diet Bread'. The description on the packaging reported that the loaf contained fifty per cent less calories than normal bread. That sounds marvellous, but, when you look at the actual loaf, the slices of bread are half the size of normal bread, which means that you'll still be hungry and you'll end up eating twice as much!

And, consequently, because you're told that you are consuming half the calories, you'll think you are on a diet and going to lose weight but, of course, you're not. You've just eaten the same amount of calories that made you fat in the first place! And then they charge you the same as a normal loaf. If you really want to lose weight, just buy normal bread and only eat half of it!!!

I call this my 'Grain of Truth'.

DINNER PARTIES

I was once asked in whose company – living or dead – I would most like to have a dinner party. I replied that I'd much rather have dinner with someone who was alive… the idea of eating next to a corpse isn't my dream night in, although they might be better company than some people I've shared a dinner table with.

But then I suppose, if I had to choose a perfect dinner party, I'd invite the following:

Jesus

He would be the obvious choice to commence proceedings by saying grace and would also be very handy to have around if we got low on drinks – what with the 'water into wine' trick. But the main reason for inviting him would be to commiserate with him for being born on Christmas Day. I actually feel very sorry for him because that must be the worst day to have your birthday and, when he was a kid, he would definitely have lost out and received only one lot of presents.

Gordon Ramsay

I must admit his swearing probably wouldn't go down very well, especially with the Son of God seated next to him, but he'd probably get so fed up and frustrated with the quality of food that was being served that he'd jump up, go into the kitchen and take over! The only drawback is that I'd probably be too scared to tell him I don't eat anything green and then have to suffer the consequences (probably spinach).

Marilyn Monroe

Not only would she add a real touch of glamour and sparkle but, if anyone had a birthday that night, she could sing a very sexy rendition of 'Happy Birthday' to them. That would save me having to perform the song and all the bother of getting dressed up as a bloody penguin, which, despite being a very fetching outfit, still wouldn't quite have the allure of Miss Monroe's birthday offering! (I dressed as a penguin for a particular hotel guest once and it has been expected of me ever since.)

Elvis

The dinner party would inevitably turn into a Party Night and so I could have an impromptu Elvis lookalike competition, which he ought to win. I'd have to make extra puddings for him, of course.

Tommy Cooper

One of my heroes! This would just be an excuse for him to entertain us with some of his favourite jokes:

'Police arrested two men yesterday. One was drinking battery acid, the other was eating fireworks. They charged one and let the other off.'

'I chopped the bottom off one of my trousers legs and put it in the library. I thought that it would be a turn-up for the books.'

'I went into this pub and I ate a ploughman's lunch. He was livid.'

Oprah Winfrey

I really admire her because she was born into poverty and has been hugely successful in everything she's done. Apart from being very intelligent, brilliant company and quite an actress, she also happens to be worth zillions of dollars. Her book club has been responsible for selling over fifty-five million copies both on TV and the Internet. I hope you don't think that I'm just having her there to plug this book. Not at all! That would be very mercenary. No, my interest in her is for another reason. One of high art and cultural aspiration. You see, she's also a film producer and I reckon she might just option the movie rights. Naturally, I'd want to play myself but, as second choice, George

Clooney is about the same age as me and I believe we share the same dentist.

Winston Churchill
He could deliver a rousing after-dinner speech and then light up the most enormous cigar. No one would dare tell him that he wasn't allowed to smoke indoors anymore – so I'd get away with being able to have a fag as well!

And last but not least…

Guy Fawkes
The evening wouldn't be complete without a great fireworks display. The thing I've never understood about Bonfire Night (although I like the cooking-the-sausages-on-a-fire bit) is that hundreds of years later we still make a big celebration of the fact that Guy Fawkes failed in his attempt to rid us once and for all of all the MPs. I can't help feeling that, if someone tried the same thing today and actually triumphed, in a few hundred years everyone would be celebrating the fact that someone actually succeeded… not bloody failed!

I haven't bothered to work out the seating plan – I'd be slightly worried that Jesus might be reminded of The Last Supper and so I'd put him at the head of the table so he could keep an eye on things. I suppose it would also be sensible to have Elvis nearest the toilet – for obvious reasons. Still, with this stellar guest list I wouldn't have to worry too much about who sits where. Let's face it, a gathering of such famous names would be wonderful. And even better – I'd be the only guest I hadn't heard of.

EASTER

Something that has never really made any sense to me is the fact that Easter is at a different time every year. I mean, we don't have all this bother with Christmas – it's 25 December and that's that; we can all plan ahead knowing exactly when it's going to be. But Easter is a bloody nightmare. It's meant to be a religious festival – surely, if we know when Jesus was born, we must know when he died!

Apparently, it's what's called a moveable feast as it doesn't fall on a fixed date in the Gregorian or Julian calendars, whatever that means, and the actual date of Easter each year is all to do with the positioning of the moon in the solar system. Apparently, this took centuries for men wiser than me to compute and caused huge controversy. That I can believe – probably why the shops start stocking Easter eggs on Boxing Day because they have no idea when it is either. It's amazing how the Easter Bunny knows when to call. Speaking of which, why do we have an Easter Bunny? I wouldn't mind but rabbits don't even lay eggs!

By the way, do you know what you call a bunny with a large brain? AN EGGHEAD!

No, none of this makes sense to me. Christmas is always on the same date, so why don't they do the same with Easter? I suggest 1 April each year is adopted as Good Friday and then we'll all know exactly where we stand. In fact, I might start a campaign as soon as I've sorted out National Smoking Day (see 'S' for SMOKING)

There was also meant to be a big star in the sky at Christmas – so I think we should have something similarly stellar (blimey, that's good alliteration) launched into the universe to celebrate Easter. I'm sure Richard Branson could arrange something suitable.

EQUALITY

Now I'm all for this equality stuff – well, in principle anyway – but I'm beginning to think it's starting to go too far the other way. It's now getting to the point where men are being discriminated against for… well, for being men. Let me explain.

During my recent Party Night Tour, I was driving back to London from Glasgow when everything went pear-shaped. It wasn't surprising because it had already been one of those evenings when things didn't go according to plan. The show hadn't gone as well as I'd hoped, being in Scotland, straight after the referendum (and, in retrospect, it probably also had something to do with all the Union Jacks I had draped all over the stage). Part of my build-up entrance music is the theme from *The Dam Busters* – but I don't know why that upset them. Barnes Wallis's 'Bouncing Bomb' wasn't used at the battle of Culloden as far as I know. But then I later discovered it had something to do with it being the Glasgow Rangers Football Club theme tune and my partygoers were mainly Celtic supporters!

Anyway, there I was happily trundling along on my way home in my rental van (just after the satnav told me to continue on the same road for 181 miles. I had no idea that we actually had any roads in this country that went on for 181 miles!), when suddenly I started to hear a very loud knocking noise coming from the engine. Blimey, I thought, this doesn't sound good. Fortunately, at that precise moment, I saw a sign for a motorway service station about a mile ahead – so, rather than immediately pulling up on the hard shoulder, I did what I thought was the sensible thing and limped along towards the service station before pulling in.

If I'm honest, I was also desperately in need of a coffee so this was perfect. It was also just starting to rain, so I drove round the service station and I managed to pull up on the petrol forecourt, parking the van under the canopy. This is all I bloody need, I thought. I was tired and grumpy – very unlike me, as you all know. All I really wanted to do was get home. But then I thought of Wing Commander Guy Gibson and those other dam-busting pilots and thought they would have remained cool, calm and collected in this situation. I must remain composed, show a stiff upper lip and not panic. At least I wasn't under enemy fire.

The van was hired, so I knew that I wouldn't be the one stuck with a hefty repair bill and that help would soon be at hand, as I'm a member of a motoring organisation. And not just any old one, no! The same illustrious one the Queen belongs to: the Royal Automobile Club!

A quick inspection of the paperwork confirmed that I was, in fact, doubly covered – by my own membership and by the van-hire people. Hooray!!! I phoned the RAC and proudly told them of my dual eligibility and that I needed help ASAP. I also informed them, with unparalleled smugness, that I had managed to park the van under the garage forecourt at the service station so the nice man coming out to see me wouldn't even have to get wet! How thoughtful was that? That sort of consideration, not to mention my duplicate registration to the RAC (have I mentioned that?), would, I assumed, encourage them to treat me as some sort of priority. Well, how wrong was I?

The bureaucrat at the other end of the line was very unhelpful – I bet he didn't even salute me like in the old days. Yes, I know he was on the phone, but some traditions should be continued whatever the circumstances, don't you think? Anyway, I was informed that, as I had managed to drive into the service-station area and wasn't actually on the hard shoulder, I was considered a 'non-priority' and, as such, I would have to wait at least ninety minutes before someone would show up. And, if they couldn't fix it there and then, as I was in a van, it would be at least another four hours-plus before they would even bother to get a truck to me to take me and the bloody van home!

I needed a break and a coffee but not that long a bloody break.

I can only assume that, if I'd have just stopped on the road and not cared about the mechanic getting soaked and having to work on the side of the road with juggernauts thundering past him on the hard shoulder, I would have been a priority case and they'd have been with me in less than forty minutes!

Clearly, that wasn't the case. Apparently, the only way to ensure you get priority assistance is to be a woman – and not just a woman but a woman on her own! Of course, I understand that the safety of the fairer sex is paramount at all times, but what gets me is that I pay the same as anyone else – in fact, in this case, technically, I'd paid double, once via the van-hire firm and again with my own membership. They should have actually come out to me twice as fast as anyone else.

What I'm going to do next year, when my membership comes up for renewal, is take out a joint membership with an imaginary wife and carry a spare set of women's clothes and some make-up with me wherever I go. That way, if I do break down, I'll phone up and tell them I'm Mrs Jenkins, explain that I've got a bit of a sore throat and, most importantly, that I'm on my own. I'll get any passengers to hide in the boot and then I'll have under forty minutes to quickly get changed and do my make-up before the nice RAC man gets to me! This scheme will also serve as a very good audition should I ever be asked to play a pantomime dame.

Oh, and by the way, when the RAC mechanic did eventually turn up, he discovered the fault straightaway and actually used superglue to fix it. The noise stopped immediately. I asked him what had caused the problem and he replied, 'I expect you've heard this before but... you've got a screw loose.' And with that, he saluted me. Unbelievable!!!

F

FAT PEOPLE

I'm not one to employ four-letter words – I believe it means
you lack imagination in your vocabulary. However, I will use
a three-letter word that a lot of people avoid using... FAT.
Yes, that's right, FAT! There are now so many euphemisms to
describe lardies in order to protect their feelings that it's become
ridiculous. Expressions such as 'Generously Proportioned',
'Oversized' and even 'Fluffy' have become the norm. While
researching this subject (Ha! If you believe that, you'll believe
anything) I've even come up with a few thoughts of my
own. How about 'Gastronomically Challenged', 'Rotundally
Vulnerable' or 'Chubbily Susceptible'?

There are also so many excuses: I once heard one human
butterball say that his fat was just muscle that was relaxing.

I'm going to get straight to the point here. To my mind, unless you have a medical condition, if you're fatter than you want to be… it's your own fault!

Of course, there are lots of excuses people give as to why they've become oversized (oh dear, now I'm using euphemisms), which usually are that it's glandular, that they are big-boned, they have a slow metabolism – but I'm afraid I can't accept these reasons.

Look at famous fat people throughout history. I can't think Henry VIII had a glandular problem – he just liked stuffing great ham hocks in his mouth. And it made him very unhappy. He probably took one look in the mirror of a morning and thought to himself, 'I've put a bit of poundage on – someone has got to pay for this.' And to cheer himself up, he decided to behead a wife or two. Bit drastic, I know… but then a man must have a hobby.

I've never understood people who moan because they've become fat. I mean, men with a 50-in waist don't suddenly wake up one morning and look down to see this giant belly hiding the view of their feet. The extra 16 inches didn't appear overnight after one giant meal. At one stage they were probably a 34-in waist – the problem was that they put on an odd inch or two, so they went out and bought larger trousers: 36-in, then 38, 40 and so on, until they were having to buy jeans that fitted a 50-in waist. It's all completely their own fault and the solution is simple: if you don't want to get fat… DON'T BUY BIGGER CLOTHES!!!

If the only trousers you own are for a 34-in waist, you'll

never become fatter than you are. And without trousers, you can't go out and buy food so then you'll never get fat!

I've known quite a few fat people – when one pal of mine walks down Oxford Street, it becomes one-way. Another old friend won't go swimming anymore because she's afraid of being harpooned.

I've also had a few broken beds in various hotels I've run – especially if it was a couple and both of them were on the large side. The most common complaint from fat people wasn't that there wasn't enough food; it was that some of the bedrooms only had showers rather than baths. Often the shower cubicles only had a small door to pass through and so they couldn't get in and wash themselves. I think this was actually more of an inconvenience for some of the other guests if the weather was really hot and they were staying for a week!

If the hotel was full and I couldn't move them to another room, I usually suggested they went down to the swimming pool and used the shower in there. Either that or there was a hose pipe outside in the car park that the coach drivers used to wash the coaches with. Some of them weren't too happy about that. I don't know why – there was always plenty of water and space for them to move around in, and they could wash their cars at the same time. Some people are just never satisfied.

Here's another thought: fat people cost the NHS a fortune – far more than smokers – so they should TAX fattening foods to discourage people from eating so much and getting so fat. And, like on cigarette packets, where they try to discourage you with pictures of black lungs and horrible-looking tumours, they should have pictures of really fat people on chocolate bars, bags of crisps and chip wrappers to warn you what will happen if you eat them. Maybe even some graphic images of liposuction. In this technical age it must be possible to stream a live tummy-tuck procedure on a packet of biscuits or display a YouTube link on an ice-cream carton to a very obese Elvis sitting on his toilet – just before… well, you know what happened.

I also think that, in supermarkets, they should put all the fattening foods in special aisles that are really narrow, so only fit and slim people can actually get to them. And, by the way, how come you never see 'Fat Clubs' that people join because they want to get fat? Judging by the number of fat people out on the streets, there must be hundreds of such institutions!

I've always taken care of my physique and eaten sensibly (nothing green) so that now I'm so thin I don't even make a shadow.

FLYING

I recently flew for the first time with one of those cheap budget airlines. I fancied a week away in the sun and I was quite excited to see just how cheap the actual flight was. Naturally, there was a catch because it was one of those companies that charge you extra to take a suitcase, which is all a bit of a con: I've always believed that taking a suitcase is fairly standard procedure if you're going on holiday somewhere.

But what really annoyed me was that the cost of checking in the suitcase was almost as much again as the cost of the bloody flight!

FLYING

I decided they weren't going to get one over on me like this so I thought I'd somehow manage without checking in any luggage. I did wonder if I could just wear everything! After all, I was going somewhere hot so I was planning on spending most days just lazing round the pool and I didn't really need many clothes. But then I realised that you are allowed to take a small case with you on the plane without paying anything extra and you don't have all the hanging around waiting and then trying to grab your suitcase as it travels round the carousel like some fairground game where you have to grab the case quickly and, if you miss it, you have to wait till it comes round again. It seemed a very good idea and, better still, it would save me some money.

Anyway, I ventured out to the shops to purchase a new case, as all my other luggage was too big. And just to make sure, I had my tape measure in hand, so that my new case conformed to the permitted size.

The other thing I had to think about and which gave me a headache was all the extra airport security and the fact that you're apparently only allowed to take so many millilitres of liquid in any one container in your hand luggage.

Unfortunately, all the items I had already purchased were too big, and so I ended up spending a small fortune buying miniatures of everything: shaving gel, deodorant, aftershave lotion, toothpaste, mouthwash, suntan lotion for my face, suntan lotion for the rest of me, shampoo and, of course, conditioner. These bloody miniatures cost the same, if not more, than normal-size ones! So, by now, with the cost of the new tiny suitcase, I realised I'd almost spent the same as if I'd paid for the normal bloody suitcase to fly with me. Blimey!

Anyway, I bought a clear plastic bag and just about succeeded in getting all my miniature bottles, pots, tubs and tubes in it. And, by wearing my jacket and a few extra items of clothing, I just managed to get everything else I needed to take in the tiny case.

As I was going through security, I put my plastic bag in the tray but it was immediately taken out. At first I thought maybe it was because I looked suspicious, as by now I was sweating profusely – mainly because I was wearing several layers of clothing (the garments that wouldn't fit in the case). The security man picked up my clear plastic bag.

'They're all little ones!' I stated proudly.

'Yes,' said the security man, 'but unfortunately, you have too many of them.'

I then stood and looked on helplessly as he confiscated half of my purchases and watched as he threw them away.

'You can replace them over there.' He pointed to the various airport shops where they sold normal-sized ones at double the price that you'd normally pay. Apparently, it's OK to take those normal-sized ones on the plane because you've bought them at the airport!

I was about to faint from all the extra layers and the cost of my various liquids. It was at this point that I started to wish I'd just paid extra and checked in my normal-sized suitcase.

I finally boarded my plane – only to be sat next to a really fat man who must have been 20 stone. The unfairness of it all suddenly hit me: in this current system of ticketing and pricing, my oversized neighbour had paid the same basic low fare as me and, even if I combined my normal-sized suitcase with my weight, it would come to nowhere near as much as he weighed in his birthday suit, which was not only unreasonable but also a horrible image!

I think what all airlines should do is charge you by weight. So never mind charging extra for checking in your case (or worse still, an extra surcharge if your case is slightly heavier than it should be), airline fares should be on a sliding scale, based on weight. They should actually charge you by the pound (lb) so that, when you check in at the airport, they put you on the scales with your suitcase. In this way, the fare would be based on your combined weight. (I think I'll write to Sir Richard Branson... again.)

And the worse thing was that the holiday was a bloody nightmare – the weather was terrible and I didn't use any of my various lotions and creams. It never stopped raining all week. All I really needed was a bloody umbrella, which, of course, was the one thing I had no intention of taking on a sunshine holiday!

I could easily have travelled much lighter... and cheaper.

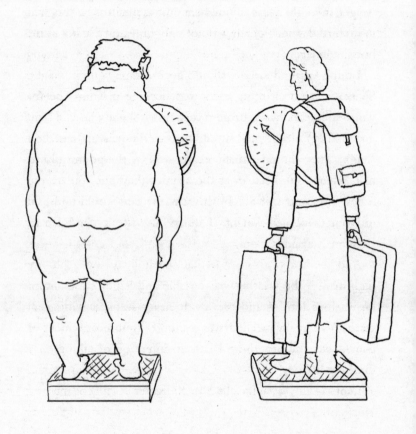

FOOTBALL

I think everyone should support their local team. I mean, it's ridiculous that you get fans who support teams miles from where they live. What about all the Liverpool supporters who hail from my neck of the woods – Torquay and further points west? Most Manchester United supporters live in Godalming, although I suppose any excuse to get out of Godalming makes sense. I once went there and it was closed. No, I really believe fans should be made to support their local team and, if I had my way, this 'rule' would extend to players as well. I mean, how can you say you have a local team when none of the players are 'local'? Half of them can't even speak English, let alone know anything about the neighbourhood. And it's not just the players; it's impossible to understand what some managers are saying because their grasp of English is so poor. And that's just Harry Redknapp.

I mean, how many Wolves players actually come from Wolves? Well, if there were a place called Wolves, I bet they wouldn't come from there. I reckon players should have to have been born in the town that they represent or at least have lived there for FIVE YEARS!!! Then you'd have a true representation of a local team. All right, it may mean that smaller towns like Hartlepool and Millwall struggle to put out a decent side and there may be trouble with EU legislation and international employment law, but, as you know, when I get an idea or have a project, I'm not someone to be put off by such notions of globalisation and the like. And anyway, they do it in cricket!

I was once invited to Torquay United for a charity event (I like to give something back as well as take) and at half time I went onto the pitch to try to hit the crossbar. I didn't think that would be too difficult until they said I had to use a football. Anyway, they gave me a microphone so I could address the crowd, which was about 3,500 strong. I began by saying, 'I'm really surprised to be here today… I didn't know Torquay still had a football team.' Well, I was about to go on to say something nice about the pies but I didn't manage to say anything else because they grabbed the mic off me before I had a chance. The boos were so loud you couldn't hear anything anyway, although I did get some loud cheers from the away supporters. As always, I was PREPARED for any such eventuality and quickly stripped off to reveal a Torquay United kit, which I'd donned under my clothes. Yellow isn't my colour and I haven't got the most muscular of legs but, I must say, it did the trick and most of the boos turned into cheers.

I've never played myself. I'd probably lose… No, I didn't mean that! It should read, I've never played, myself. If I had to be involved, I'd like to be the referee. I don't understand any of the rules of the game but that doesn't seem to be a drawback for most referees. Although I'm by no means a fan of dictatorships (see 'P' for POLITICS), I like the idea of being dressed in black, waving my arms about, giving orders and blowing on a gleaming Acme Thunderer (that's a whistle, by the way). But another thing – and probably the most important – is that referees don't have to share a dressing room. Now I'm in showbiz, I've learned that things like that are important. In fact, if I were a footballer earning millions a year, I'd insist on it. I'm actually very surprised that they don't!

G

GARDENING

You may wonder why I've chosen gardening as a topic when I tell you that, if I'm honest, I don't really know much about the subject, apart from the fact that 'Roses are Red and Violets are Blue' and I learned that from a Valentine's card and not from attending the Chelsea Flower Show.

But I do know how much gardeners charge per hour. Well, at least I did know a few years ago, back when I not only had a garden but, more importantly, could afford to pay a gardener! I once asked him what he put on his rhubarb. He replied, 'Horse manure.' I told him that was funny because I preferred custard!

I wish I did know more about pottering about in flowerbeds and rockeries, although, having a natural dislike of all things green, I'm not sure that I would want to end up with green fingers! In fact, the only way I can tell the difference between a weed and a valuable plant is when I pull on it. If it doesn't move, it's a weed and, if I'm able to pull it up easily, it means it's a valuable plant! I'd also like to know who actually made the decision as to which are plants and which are weeds. Probably the Queen or Alan Titchmarsh.

Since giving up the hotel business, I'm fortunate enough to be living on a farm – although it's not actually my farm. The idea of getting up at 5 am to milk the cows and then muck out the horses has never really appealed to me for some reason – well, for many reasons, actually. However, living on a farm does have its advantages: aside from not needing an alarm clock (the bloody cockerel does that job), if the grass starts to get a bit long in the nearby field, the sheep suddenly appear as if by magic and start munching away and do the job much better than a lawnmower.

It must be really odd being a sheep and only eating grass (as you know, it certainly wouldn't suit me). Imagine living a life completely surrounded by food as far as the eye can see. I suppose at least grass isn't fattening! By the way, did you know it apparently takes three sheep just to make one jumper? That really surprised me… I didn't even know sheep could knit!

People do become obsessed with their gardens and end up behaving somewhat eccentrically. Prince Charles is quite famous for talking to flowers – I suppose it's quite nice when you're rattling around in a palace to have some company. Although I live alone I haven't yet started conversations with my poinsettias. Actually, I can't even look after my house plants properly and, when I was away doing panto, I thought I'd give them all enough water to last while I was away for the month. Of course, when I came home, they had all died! Most of the water was still in the pots – apparently, I'd overwatered them and they'd drowned. Perhaps I should have explained to them to try not to drink all the water in one go!

No, I don't think gardening's for me. As you know, I'm not one to give up easily but, in this case, I think I'll throw in the trowel.

GIRLFRIENDS

When I was about eleven years old, I managed to get my first proper girlfriend. She was called Liz. (She was no relation to the Queen, obviously, although I do like regal names and, in fact, all my children are named after royalty.) Liz and I didn't go to the same school and we actually met because she lived just down the road from me.

She also seemed much older than me… well, it seemed so at the time because she was twelve, going on thirteen. I thought she was out of my league but, when she agreed to go out with me, I was ecstatically happy. At the age of eleven it seemed to be a brilliant achievement – quite a feather in my cap to be going out with an 'older woman'! I thought she was gorgeous; she was really slim and had long blonde hair all down her back – none on her head, just down her back! (Sorry – I just couldn't resist putting that old gag in!) I've always had a thing for blondes. Probably my downfall. (See 'M' for MARRIAGES.)

Anyway, I thought she was really lovely and we spent quite a lot of time in each other's company, mainly playing in the park together after school. But there was a problem: not only was she a bit older than me but also I was a bit of a slow developer – thinking about it, I'm still waiting to grow a bit more now! Like lots of girls at that age, Liz was a fast developer and she was a bit taller than me.

To be totally honest, she was quite a lot taller than me, to the point that, if we spent a lot of time staring into each other's eyes romantically, she was either going to develop a stoop or I'd end up with a stiff neck. I mean, it's nice to have a girlfriend that you can look up to, but this was a bit too much. I originally thought she was out of my league, but she was actually out of my reach!

To compensate for this and to make it more comfortable when we went out for a walk holding hands, I had the ideal solution. It was brilliant in its simplicity: I would stroll along the pavement and make her walk in the gutter. Fantastic. That way, it gave us the appearance of being the same height and we didn't look quite so ill matched. Liz didn't seem to mind and it worked fine, apart from the times when it rained and buses went thundering past and soaked her.

Liz seemed a good sport and I was sure that she was happy with this arrangement as well as the relationship, which I thought would last forever – or at least until the end of the summer term. Unfortunately, I was wrong. It turned out Liz was a bit too much of a 'good sport' and, after a few weeks, she dumped me and went off with someone else at school. I can only assume he was probably a bit taller, more handsome and dashing than me… and someone who didn't make her walk in the gutter.

They say size isn't everything – unfortunately, with my first girlfriend, it appears it was!

If only the relationship had lasted until the following year it wouldn't have been such a problem. You see, that was the year platform shoes became all the rage for men and by then I was working sixty hours a week in the school holidays. I had saved up and bought myself a pair of amazing platform boots with 6-in heels and 4-in soles and I was instantly 6 inches taller!

Unfortunately, this fashion revolution didn't help me in my quest for a new girlfriend because platform shoes became all the rage for girls as well… and so they all instantly grew by another 6 inches. Although the shoes helped me overcome my shortcomings, they really didn't help when it came to finding romance.

THE WORLD ACCORDING TO MANAGER MARK

GLASSES

I wear glasses for reading these days but there was a time when I had to wear them for everything. In fact, I first started wearing spectacles at just eighteen months old and, because I had a lazy eye, I spent half the time wearing a patch over one eye. I must have looked like a mini Long John Silver (maybe that would be a Short John Silver).

As I got older, school photographs were a nightmare: either I couldn't be seen because the flash hitting the lenses resulted in a blinding explosion of light, or the photographer would pull the glasses down my nose so far and twist them so that in the photo the position of the frames made it appear that I didn't actually have any eyes!

The only good thing was that the spectacles I wore worked for reading as well as normal seeing. Then, a few years ago, the optician informed me that I'd need to start wearing two pairs of glasses. I was wondering how one pair would fit over the other until he explained that they weren't to be worn at the same time! One pair was for day-to-day living and the other for reading (not books, obviously). The alternative was to have bifocals, which I thought was some kind of folding door and, because I didn't want to move house, I turned that offer down.

I didn't fancy all the bother of switching glasses and, as I'd seen adverts for laser surgery, I thought maybe that this could be an option. The ads claimed the cost to be from £700 (unfortunately, per eye), so off I went for a consultation – only to be told it would cost me £3,500! I'd been called 'four eyes' before but now it looked like they were going to charge me for five eyes!

I never actually discovered why they upped my costs so exorbitantly. They must have seen me coming (in my Bentley). They told me that, while I wouldn't need glasses for everyday use, I would still need them for reading. That's OK, I thought, I can manage with one pair.

The procedure was to be carried out in Bristol and I arranged for someone to go with me, as I was advised that I wouldn't be able to drive myself home. I was expecting a plush private hospital but my satnav guided us to a large shopping centre out of town, where I found myself waiting in a very crowded opticians while hordes of shoppers peered at us through the window. I suppose it must be some sort of spectator sport in Bristol. Not what I expected for forking out £3,500!

About forty minutes after my due appointment time, my name was finally called and I was led off to a room where some drops were put in my eyes. It bloody stung, I can tell you, and I was sitting there, tears flowing – from the pain, not the fear, before you think I'm a wimp. (I'm quite good with pain – I used to have my hair cut without an anaesthetic.) Anyway, then there was further discussion because my pupils weren't getting big enough and so I was given even more drops. To be fair, my eyes were already so sore it didn't hurt so much the second time. Eventually… success! I was ready to go into the operating room.

I had to sit in a chair, which was a bit like an oversized dentist chair, and found myself being tipped back before being raised as far as the seat would go. I told them I wasn't very good with heights but they took no notice of me. Then before I knew it (well, actually I did know it because I saw them), two men in masks appeared. At first I thought that I was about to be robbed but was then assured they were going to perform the procedure. I can only assume they wear masks so that, if anything goes wrong, you won't know who to blame!

To begin with, they attached this device that somehow holds your eye wide open with your top eyelid wrapped round it. And, yes, it is even more uncomfortable than it sounds! Then more drops are squirted in your eye to numb them and… after a few minutes… IT STARTS! This futuristic, large machine, which wouldn't have been out of place in the control room of the *Starship Enterprise*, starts to bear down and you're told to look directly at the light.

Then you hear this noise and start to feel a really dull pain in a weird place, right at the back of your eyeball. Then the worst bit of all… you can smell burning. Yes, BURNING!!! But it's only when you realise that the smell of burning is, in fact, the laser BURNING OUT YOUR EYEBALL that you fully comprehend that you're the starring role in your own horror movie. Have you seen *The Texas Chainsaw Massacre*? Well, it's obviously not as gruesome as that, but it's still bad.

Anyway, this goes on for what seems like an eternity until they finally stop lasering you.

Phew! It's over! You breathe a sigh of relief as they take off the device that was holding your eye open. You can breathe again and think of the future and how much you've got to live for and thank God or whoever that it's all over. But then you hear the chilling words of the optician... A simple sentence that strikes terror into your heart: 'Right, now let's get started on the other eye.'

Unbelievable!!!

GLOBAL CREDIT CRUNCH

I've been blamed for many things but I can honestly say the global credit crunch wasn't my fault!

The whole thing is nonsense anyway. When coins and paper money were first invented, you could only print to the value of the gold your country had. The clue is in the fact that it used to say, 'I promise to pay the bearer on demand.' In fact, money was invented as an IOU for gold but, like most countries, we sold off all our gold years ago, so now money is just worthless pieces of paper. It doesn't really exist: an IOU that could never be honoured. If you think about it, every time a bank lends out a loan for a mortgage, in order to do so, they'd have to have someone walk into their branch with a suitcase stuffed full of money! Of course, that doesn't happen... the money they lend you doesn't really exist.

The entire wealth of the modern world is actually built on useless IOUs that could never be cashed. When the credit crunch happened, banks lost confidence in each other, so the governments stepped in and replaced the worthless bank IOUs with worthless IOUs of their own... which they could only do if they wrote more IOUs as a country!

As a nation, we pay a huge amount of extra tax every

year towards settling the national debt, but why bother? We never really borrowed anything because it was never there to borrow… we just wrote out a load of IOUs. If every country just tore up the IOUs, we'd all be free from debt and could just start again with much lower taxes and the world would be a much better place!

HOORAY!!!

GONGS

I'm not talking dinner gongs or those huge resounding orchestral gongs – the type that Bombardier Billy Wells used to bash before Rank films (and by the way, 'Rank' in those days didn't mean 'rotten' – Rank was a film company). No, I mean the CBEs, OBEs and the MBEs awarded to deserving public servants, hardworking citizens and actors.

There are various Orders of the British Empire, including Order of the Garters (must be for strippers and lap dancers), Knighthoods, Commanders and the like, but my favourite (and the one thing I did learn in panto) – there is nothing like a Dame!

I'm delighted to see dinner ladies, lollipop people and street cleaners become recognised for their services to the public but there have been some ridiculous awards to already rich people just for doing their jobs. It's also unfair that film stars and the like presumably have various homes around the world in which to exhibit their medals but I expect poor people's lack of space means they have to store their medals in the outside toilet, where only a select few invited guests can admire them.

Of course, 'gongs' can also apply to film, television and theatrical awards. What about the Oscar ceremony? Some of those acceptance speeches are totally cringeworthy and I can't bear all that gushing, mutual schmoozing and self-congratulation. Having said that, I'd love to be there one day to experience the glamour, glitz and Hollywood atmosphere. I also have to admit, if asked, I'd be delighted to take Julia Roberts up the red carpet.

No, I don't suppose an Oscar is likely to head my way and a BAFTA is, I admit, a long shot. Although I did attend the BAFTA Television Awards a few years ago (I wasn't there for an award, I just went along so I'd know where to go if I do ever finally get one!) and the following January, much to my surprise, my appearance that night on the red carpet was even shown on *ITV News at Ten*! Unfortunately, it wasn't about me – the only reason I was featured was because I just happened to be stood alongside Sienna Miller and they showed some footage with me in shot (the actual news report was about phone hacking).

There is one other possibility, of course: if, by any chance, you are reading this, Your Majesty, and, before you get on to your very own section ('Q' for QUEEN, of course), there have been relatively few medals awarded to the hotel and tourist industry. So, if you're ever in the position where you need to find a place for some unclaimed gongs, please think of me. I'd be honoured to receive a Royal Tweet at any time of the day or night.

GREETINGS CARDS

There was a time when greetings cards were reserved mainly just for birthdays and, of course, Christmas. Oh, and Mother's

Day, which is often exactly nine months after Father's Day. There are anniversary cards, get-well cards, moving-house cards – those are tricky to send because, when people move, you don't always know where to send them!

According to some sources (soy?), it was the Chinese who used to exchange goodwill messages in order to celebrate the New Year. Of course, they have their own New Year, which is different to ours and isn't celebrated on 1 January. Their New Year begins on a different day each year, which must be very confusing for them and explains why they don't sing 'Auld Lang Syne' on 31 December – a shame, although at least they don't have to listen to bagpipes.

But now the whole thing has become absolutely ridiculous because they make cards for every occasion. I understand sympathy cards (a good way of getting out of going to funerals) but what is the point of 'friendship' cards. If you're friends with someone, you don't need to send them a card to say so – they already know it – and if they aren't aware, you can't really be good friends. And what with the ever increasing costs of cards and the price of stamps, it's much better to buy a friend something that bonds you together… like a tube of UHU, for example.

There are cards for grandparents, bosses, secretaries, teachers – everyone, in fact – and the greetings card companies have even invented days that don't exist just to sell more cards: it wouldn't surprise me to learn they do cards that say 'Sorry Your Pet Died Day'. And what about greetings such as, 'Sorry You're Leaving' and 'Sorry You're Not Leaving' (well, OK, they probably don't have that one yet but it won't be long coming, believe me!)?

In fact, thinking about it, I'm surprised they don't do a whole range of 'non-greetings cards' to send to people you don't like, such as in the cartoon film of *Alice in Wonderland* when they sang 'A very merry un-birthday to you!' I can think of a few people I'd like to send one of those to.

Oh, and I haven't even mentioned Valentine's Day cards yet.

When I was younger, I really fancied this girl I worked with at the local bingo hall. I was the caller and she was the checker and I'd wanted to mark her card for some time! Talk about Legs Eleven… I'd given her Kelly's Eye for a while, hoping I'd be her number one and was getting in a bit of a two and eight each time I saw her. The trouble is I'd blush whenever I had to call out number 'forty-four' (that's one for the bingo enthusiasts among my readers!)

Anyway, we were both single and, being a bit of a romantic, I decided to buy her a Valentine's card – not just any Valentine's card but a great big giant one! It was actually about 4-ft tall – almost as tall as I was, and far too large to post. Because it was such a ridiculous size, I didn't want to embarrass her by leaving it somewhere at work. But I knew where she lived and so I came up with a cunning plan…

I knew she'd probably be at home at a certain time on the morning of Valentine's Day and I had originally thought about sneaking up her driveway, ringing the bell, leaving it on the door step and running away! But I was worried I'd get caught, so I nipped down to the local taxi rank and asked a cabbie to deliver it for me! It was going to cost me a bit more but

I thought it was a brilliant plan and I really liked her – so I thought she was definitely worth the extra expense! And even more importantly, she'd have no idea who it was from. And before you ask, no, I didn't have the nerve to sign the card!

All that I'd put at the bottom of the card after the soppy Valentine's message (mine, not Hallmark's) was a big question mark.

Anyway, I gave the cabbie the card and off he went to deliver this special missive. I spent the next few hours rather excited and nervous. I knew I'd be seeing her later that day at work and couldn't wait to discover what she thought about it.

I went into work rather anxiously but also with a 'clickety-click' in my step. I saw her from a distance and was about to approach her in a nonchalant, blasé, devil-may-care sort of way and talk about the weather or something like that but, as soon as she saw me, she came straight over and said, 'Oh, thank you for the card!'

'But… but how did you know it was from me?' I asked.

'Well,' my paramour replied, 'My nan answered the door and so I asked her who delivered it and she said, "Some bloke with glasses and a moustache."'

Oh blimey! At the time I wore glasses and had a moustache… I hadn't noticed that the bloody taxi driver I'd asked to deliver the card also had a moustache and wore glasses and so she assumed it was me that had brought it over. Unbelievable!

So there was no intrigue or surprise but she was impressed and my massive Valentine's card did the trick (you see, size does matter). Well, at least for a while… because this girl went on to become wife number one! So we did actually set up 'Housey House' for a while!

Sadly, the marriage didn't work. I have a suggestion for those greetings card manufacturers. Perhaps they should make Happy Divorce cards – I'd probably end up buying those in bulk.

H

HONEYMOONS

My most expensive holidays have always been my honeymoons. Not the actual cost of the trip but I'm including the expense of the wedding and then the inevitable divorce. I knew one couple whose reception lasted longer than the marriage. Not that I'm saying marriages always end in divorce – but mine always do. Whereas most couples have a sixty per cent chance of being successful, I have a 100 per cent failure rate.

I did go to SANDALS resort in Jamaica. (I've put this in CAPITALS in case this is what they call product placement. If so, any chance of a free holiday, Mr SANDALS?) Well, anyway, I paid a bloody fortune for the trip and it worked out at over £1,000 a night. That price did, however, include our own butler and they gave us a special mobile phone to contact him

85

every time we wanted something. I can't remember ringing him much, although my wife seemed to be quite demanding of his services.

We did have our own beachfront bungalow and it was marvellous stepping straight out onto the sand and hearing the waves pounding the shore at night. Not so good, however, when there was a high tide and the whole place flooded. You could actually dangle your feet over the sides of the bed to paddle! It was like being in *The Poseidon Adventure* with my wife playing the part of Shelley Winters.

Being an incurable romantic and despite paying a fortune for this 'all-inclusive' trip, I decided, on the first night of our honeymoon, to fork out extra to eat in the poshest restaurant in the place. Although we had only arrived that day, I had already hit the beach to 'soak up the rays'. And as I was getting ready, I noticed that the tops of my feet were already a bit sunburned and quite sore. In fact, my 'plates' did actually resemble two uncooked steaks. My socks were going to rub against them and so, to ease the pain, I decided to wear my sandals to the restaurant without any socks.

But when we got there, the staff refused to let me in because I was wearing SANDALS. My wife was wearing sandal-type shoes, as were most of the women in the restaurant, and that didn't seem to be a problem but I wasn't allowed in. I'm all for Women's Rights and everything but this was equality gone mad. Why are women allowed to show their feet but not men?!? I wouldn't have minded quite so much but, to rub salt in my already wounded feet, the bloody resort was called SANDALS!

And yet they wouldn't let me in because that's what I was wearing. Unbelievable!!!

P.S. Mr SANDALS, just in case you are reading this, I am not criticising your wonderful, exclusive, luxurious resort and I am available for a return visit – but this time on my own.

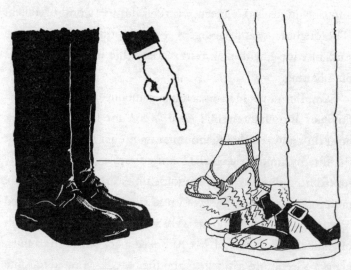

HORSES

There was a time way back before cars were invented that horses were the only way to travel, unless you boarded a pony. Nowadays, the only pony most of us will travel on will be 'Shanks's pony', which, apparently, isn't a pony at all: it's actually a description of using your own legs and walking; something I prefer not to do!

I much prefer driving, although it's interesting to note that a car's performance is still rated in comparison to horses.

Apparently, my Bentley produced the same power as 552 horses, which sounds impressive but less so when you learn that it isn't just horsepower but brake horsepower, known as bhp! Can you imagine horses with their brakes on? I didn't even know horses had brakes!

When we think of horses today, the first thought that comes into our minds isn't a means of travel but the world of 'fillies', 'Thoroughbreds' and 'gee-gees' – descriptions of racehorses. And, of course, with racecourses comes the inevitable pastime of… betting.

Now, I'm not one to encourage gambling, unless it involves dolphins and children, of course (see 'I' for INFLATABLES), but I do know a little bit about it; my brother was a bookie for a while, my auntie had several betting shops and, after my father retired from showbiz, he spent some time earning his living as a professional gambler. He went on to run bingo halls and ended up running several casinos as well. So you could say there's a bit of gambling in my blood. My dad liked a bet but wasn't a mug. He once went into a butcher's and the butcher pointed to some beef hanging from the rack and said, 'I bet you can't touch that meat.' 'No thanks,' Dad replied. 'The steaks are too high!'

Believe it or not, it is possible to beat the bookies and win more than you lose but there is obviously a knack; while bookies take bets on every race, the secret is that, as a gambler, you don't have to! You can pick and choose what race to speculate on.

So many times, you'll see a punter spend hours studying course conditions, the jockey's record and horse's previous results in order to find that 'dead cert', only to see the horse lose. Instead of repeating the research and taking their time to study 'form', the punter is desperate to instantly win some of his money back and will then frantically place another bet in the next race – on any old nag just because he likes the horse's name!

The secret is restraint. Of course, the real overall winners of every horse race are the bookies themselves – not to mention the jockeys, who get paid win or lose. Although my height and weight would give me an advantage, I've never really fancied being a jockey. Those silk outfits are a bit garish and not me at all – although I have occasionally been complimented on my pink polka-dot pyjamas. I've also never known quite what to do with a whip.

Between you and me, despite my interest in horses, I'm not really a lover of the beasts and the thought of riding one scares me half to death. In fact, I've never actually done it. The nearest I ever came was when I was little and my parents entered me into a racing event. It wasn't exactly the Grand National or The Derby, although it was a Derby of sorts – a Donkey Derby on the beach!

It was quite an occasion, with a large crowd and a tense atmosphere before the off. I remember loads of tic-tac men shouting the odds, although they may have been deck-chair attendants trying to collect their dues.

Anyway, the steward set us off and I got a brilliant start. I took the lead and managed to stay in front throughout. It was great and I felt like a young Lester Piggott, until the final stretch. I was almost past the winning post when, for no reason, my donkey suddenly stopped in its tracks and ducked its head.

Unfortunately, having no idea about donkey behaviour, I really wasn't expecting this to happen and was flung out of the saddle, soaring over his head, ending up in a heap on the ground. But I had crossed the winning line. I had come first. I had won!

Unfortunately, the donkey had stayed where he was and hadn't finished the race. There was a Stewards Enquiry and I was disqualified. In my mind, I had actually won the race but it didn't count – apparently, you had to be on the donkey when you passed the finishing line and not flying solo through the air. I was disqualified and placed last. And that was me finished with the 'Sport of Kings'!

HOTELS

When *The Hotel* television series first aired, there was much press coverage describing my hotel as a modern-day *Fawlty Towers*, with me being dubbed the new Basil Fawlty. Bit of a cheek, I thought! For a start, Basil is much taller than me and I have more hair but the main difference between us is that Basil didn't really like his guests, whereas I did. Well… most of them!

At the beginning of filming my first series, I was asked if I'd ever stay at my own hotel, which I thought was a bit of a daft question. I was, after all, at The Grosvenor for fifty weeks of the year so why on earth would I spend my two-week holiday there as well! Of course, I didn't actually say that. No, my actual reply was much worse and sparked some controversy! What I said was, 'Well, put it this way, do you think that the owners or directors of Primark walk round dressed in Primark clothes? Probably not!'

Many described that as my 'Ratner' moment! For those of you who don't know, Gerald Ratner was the boss of what was once the biggest chain of jewellers in the UK with 1,500 shops. That was until one day when he publicly stated the only reason he was able to sell something so cheap was because it was 'utter crap'... His entire company collapsed almost overnight!

Luckily, my empire – well, all right, my hotel – didn't collapse because it wasn't 'crap'. It was simply 'budget'. You see, I was used to 5-star luxury holidays so, when I went on holiday, why would I want to stay in a budget 3-star hotel? I bet when Billy Butlin went on holiday, he didn't stay in one of his chalets in Skegness, surrounded by slot machines and redcoats. So why would I do something similar in my hotel?

Although I like staying in 5-star hotels, I've also spent my fair share of time in some ropey ones over the years. I once stayed in a hotel where business was so bad they had to steal towels from the guests! I remember that it was so dirty, you had to wipe your feet on the way out.

I really wanted to run a better class of hotel. I knew The Grosvenor wasn't the best and so I wanted to try and make up for it by ensuring that the guests all had a good time. My aim was to give them the kind of memorable holiday experiences that I enjoyed as a child. I actually did like my guests, and watching them enjoying themselves and having a wonderful holiday was the bit I loved the most. For me, while I was in the hotel business, it was really the staff that was the biggest problem!

Some of the employees were just useless and lazy – and those were the good ones! The guests were sometimes more useful than the staff and so half the time I thought that the only difference between them was that the staff picked up a bloody wage packet at the end of the week!

And I'm afraid to say that some of them were just plain dim – or in hotel parlance, 'one KitKat short of a mini-bar'. I can remember once asking a barman who'd just started working for me for a 'Pot of Tea' and to bring it through to my office, where I was having an important meeting with someone. A few minutes later he came in carrying JUST A TEAPOT! No cups, saucers, teaspoons, milk or sugar. He hadn't put it on a tray. He just stood there, holding a teapot in his hand – I'm surprised he'd even had the imagination to put in a couple of tea bags. Un-bloody-believable!!!

I was once quoted as saying that I wish I could clone myself, then I could just sack everyone and do everything myself. Not that I'm a control freak – I just like things done properly and at least I'd know to include cups when making a pot of tea!

I introduced as much entertainment as I could in my hotels to keep the guests happy – wrestling events, karaoke, even 'Hen Nights' with topless butlers. And there were the legendary Party Nights featuring games such as French Bingo, Inflatable Dolphin Racing and the balloon game, 'Who's Got the Biggest?', which have now become global successes and feature in my infamous nationwide Party Nights. I'm sorry if you think that this is too early in the book for a plug but I can't wait for 'P' for PLUG – it would be about a hundred pages in and you might have lost interest in the whole thing by then!

In my quest to make things better, while filming was going

on, I did get myself into trouble a few times! I remember calling in a hotel inspector for some advice and, while we kept him talking, we did a quick sixty-minute makeover on his bedroom (a trick of the trade I'd seen done on the telly and believed to be a great idea!). I thought it would be a nice touch to put some fresh flowers in his room but the local florist was closed – well, I actually didn't bother to check – and knowing that the hotel gardens didn't have flowers, I quickly nipped out into the adjoining local park and helped myself to a few blooms.

Blimey! That caused a stir. Talk about overreacting! You'd have thought I was as much of a public menace as Edward Scissorhands! Apparently, one man wrote in stating that I should be prosecuted and that he'd videoed the particular episode as evidence! Unbelievable! Torquay council even held a meeting to discuss it but, eventually, decided not to prosecute me as it would only give me more publicity. Well, that certainly didn't work…

It wasn't even enough for a whole bouquet and I only cut down three flowers. I treated them properly too. I snipped them off carefully with a pair of scissors, causing no damage to the remaining bunch. I was actually doing the council's work with some careful pruning. And I reckoned that the amount of money I was paying in Council Tax on the business rate meant I'd paid for the bloody things ten-times over anyway!

No, what makes a good holiday is when you do things you wouldn't normally do. I can recall years ago I went to some resort somewhere and ended up riding on a camel. Now, I didn't go on holiday to ride on a camel – it wasn't something I intended to do – but I ended up riding a camel and it created a lasting memory and that, to me, is what a good holiday is all about – a lasting memory.

I wanted to recreate something memorable like that for a special 'Family Fun Day' and so decided to borrow some alpacas. It was actually quite simple – just what I needed. There was no need to panic about procuring another animal – in fact, there was no cause for a llama! It was a bit of a struggle, initially, getting the alpacas into the hotel – the lobby was definitely not 'alpaca friendly' and, as the steps down to the garden were a bit steep (apparently, alpacas are scared of heights and subject to vertigo), I decided to put them in the lift. Apparently, an animal-rights group complained that I had transported several alpacas in this manner but, as I explained, 'The only reason I did this was because I couldn't get any camels!'

To be honest, camels would have been a much tighter squeeze, in which case the animal protesters might then have had something to bloody complain about.

People often ask me if I miss being in the hotel business and I tell them yes and no. Yes, I do miss the guests and the great holiday atmosphere… but no when it comes to employing the staff and all the other hassles that go with it.

HYPERMARKETS

As if going shopping to a supermarket wasn't confusing enough! I've always been a firm believer that too much choice is actually a bad thing. (See 'L' for LETTUCE and the fact that supermarkets now have an entire aisle just for them. If you're reading this book properly and turning the pages from left to right, you wouldn't know about LETTUCE yet, unless you're a 'flicker', in which case you run the risk of missing out the best bits. Apparently, they do that sort of thing in China: they read books back to front – i.e., from right to left – but, as this isn't written in Chinese, that's unlikely, unless, of course, it becomes a world bestseller and it's published in China. In which case I won't bother to explain where you're going wrong.)

Yes… anyway… so why anybody would want to go shopping in a hypermarket is beyond me. I've often spent what has felt like days wandering round a supermarket just trying to find a simple thing like a bag of sugar; I just don't understand why they don't put it next to the jars of coffee where it clearly and obviously belongs.

One of my pet hates when going shopping is the fact that I'm no longer trusted with the trolley and I'm made to pay a £1 deposit. I mean, do I look like the sort of person who's going to run off with the trolley and use it to wheel all my shopping home? It's interesting to note that the more upmarket supermarkets like Waitrose don't inflict this on their customers. But then again, the type of person who can afford to shop at Waitrose is less likely to run off with the trolley!

There does seem to be some sort of sport or hobby whereby people dump supermarket trolleys in the nearest canal, but you'd never catch me doing that – I have a fear of water (I'm actually not that keen on the other elements, such as air and fire, and I'm particularly uncomfortable about earth).

If I'm honest, I've never actually been to a hypermarket. I can only assume that the trolleys are twice the size of the normal ones. Maybe the idea is that shoppers are nowadays split into three groups: mini-markets are for the very thin people who don't eat much, supermarkets are for average people and, of course, the hypermarkets are where obese people shop!

HYPOCHONDRIA

Thanks to my strict regimen of no vegetables, smoking and very little exercise, I enjoy pretty good health. But the trouble is that I often think I'm about to be struck down with some serious illness or a rare condition only known to three physicians worldwide. The other morning I got a terrible shock when I woke up to find my feet had turned bright blue... then I remembered I'd forgotten to take my socks off before I went to bed.

And the trouble is, doctors don't always give you much time or reassurance. When I last visited my GP, I told her that I had hurt my arm in several places. All she said was, 'Well, don't go there anymore!'

Unbelievable!

It's not just a physical illness that I am concerned about. I am a bit of a worrier, too. I'm better now but I used to be very self-conscious – I never liked to watch rugby matches because I thought that the scrum was just an opportunity for all the players to get together and talk about me... even my tennis racquet was highly strung.

The difficulty these days is that it's so easy to go on the Internet and self-diagnose all your ailments. You can find out so much: I recently discovered muscles I didn't know existed that I was sure to pull one day and that aches and pains could develop in places I didn't know I had places. It gave me a headache!

At one point I did think about joining Hypochondriacs Anonymous. I was on my way to the meeting and got as far as the door but I then heard someone sneeze and so I went home. You can't be too careful.

But my favourite acknowledgement of hypochondria – and voted the nation's favourite epitaph – is the inscription on Spike Milligan's gravestone, which reads, 'I told you I was ill.'

I

INFLATABLES

For some reason, I'm often associated with inflatables! Actually, the main reason is that I am the creator of the globally popular 'Dolphin Racing'. I also very proudly came up with the now world-famous catchphrase that began proceedings: 'Mount Your Dolphins!'

For those few of you who haven't heard of Dolphin Racing, this was an event I used to organise in the swimming pools at my hotels. Children would perch precariously as 'jockeys' on the backs of large inflatable dolphins, while their sometimes-anxious parents stood at the far end of the swimming pool with a rope between their legs that was attached to the dolphin. The adults had to wind in the inflatables and, naturally, the first dolphin – still carrying a 'jockey' – to reach the end of the pool was the winner. Hooray! Of course, the children would often fall off and there was a lot of splashing, noise, bodies flying everywhere and general mayhem. Sometimes it resembled a scene at the Aintree Racecourse and made the infamous 'Foinavon' Grand National look like an amateur dressage event. (Well, obviously, there was no splashing at the horse race but bear with me. I'm trying to paint a picture here.)

And to make it even more interesting for the crowd of spectators, I'd set up a special Tote-betting operation so they could have a flutter and bet on the eventual winner of the race. Many a child's holiday was ruined when they were scolded for falling off and subsequently losing their parents a small fortune by not being able to remount. In fact, sometimes the adults were to blame as, in desperation, they pulled the rope too hard or too quickly and the poor child would end up in the water.

Personally, I'd like to see Inflatable Dolphin Racing as an Olympic sport. There are, after all, great advantages: it's a brilliant spectator sport – certainly more exciting to watch than the 100-metre sprint, which is all over in seconds; there's no cheating – dolphins are known far and wide for their upstanding morals; and they don't take steroids – I know this for a fact as none of my dolphins has ever failed a drugs test. To my mind, the whole thing has more porpoise to it than other sports.

As part of my recent Party Night Tour I devised a game that involved lots of inflatables and was amazed to learn that nowadays almost everything imaginable comes in such a form. You can get stags heads, ice creams, boats, castles and even large Zeppelins. Of course, inflatable women are, I gather, very popular with certain types. I've never resorted to such measures: I've already had two disastrous marriages, so I'm not very good with women – and especially those full of hot air!

But I really got a shock when I discovered that you can procure an INFLATABLE SHEEP. Why and what on earth?!? I mean, not being able to get a girlfriend is one thing but, if you can't even get a real sheep and have to settle for an inflatable one, you really have got problems!

By the way, a good tip if you do want to attract a real sheep is to keep a jar of mint sauce about your person.

INSURANCE

If I'm honest, I'm not a great lover of insurance companies. I've always felt that most of them aren't much different to betting shops in that what you are actually doing is having a bit of a wager on whether something bad is going to happen or not. The only difference is that, if you place a bet at the bookies and you win, they don't have a whole team of people investigating the details on the betting slip to see if they can get out of paying you. So, on that basis, in my opinion, most bookies – even the backstreet ones – are far more honest than most insurance companies!

Of course, the 'dead-cert' and 'odds-on' favourite bet is life insurance. What you're basically doing is having a bet on when you are going to die! The good news is that, if you take out a life policy, it is guaranteed that you'll eventually be on to a winner and you will receive a nice big fat cheque. The negative is that, the longer you live, the less likely you are to make an actual profit from the amount you've stumped up in premiums. And, of course, the real drawback and main problem with this is that you, personally, won't be around to benefit from the bloody payout!

Many of the insurance companies are extremely 'generous' and offer to double the amount they pay you in the event of accidental death! That's all very well but I'm not about to commit suicide (especially as they have a clause that stops payout if you do) and I certainly have no plans to die on bloody purpose. Thinking about it, I have no plans to actually die at all and so, whenever and however it happens, as far as I'm concerned, it will be a bloody accident!

Insurance companies, like bookies, have most bases covered and another excuse for not paying up is when they consider the claim to be the result of an 'Act of God'. It's an actual legal term for 'an unforeseeable natural phenomenon' or something for which no one can be held responsible – such as a hurricane, an earthquake or Elton John's hair.

It's actually got nothing to do with 'God' himself (if you're a feminist, that's 'herself' – although, if you are a feminist, I think you may have picked this book up by mistake), otherwise, if you could blame God for your loss, you'd have to issue a lawsuit or writ against the Creator himself, which might be tricky to serve without the right connections or people in high places!

Car insurance, which, of course, is mandatory, is also another major income earner for the companies. Believe it or not, I do have a little sympathy for them when you look at some of the claims and the excuses. Here are some of my favourites:

• 'I collided with a stationary truck coming the other way.'
• 'I left for work this morning at 7 am as usual when I drove into a bus. It wasn't my fault – the bus was five minutes early.'
• 'The other motorist was driving all over the road. I had to swerve a number of times before I hit him.'
• 'I didn't think the speed limit applied after midnight.'
• 'The accident only happened because I had one eye on the lorry in front, one eye on the cyclist and the other on the car behind.'
• 'I started to turn around and it was then that I noticed a

camel and an elephant tethered on the pavement. I was
naturally distracted, lost concentration and hit a bollard.'

Of course, you can insure yourself against anything, even damage
to a specific part of your body. In the 1940s, at the request of
her film studio, actress Betty Grable had her legs insured for $1
million each; twenty years on, restaurant critic Egon Ronay had
his taste buds insured; and, more recently, comedian Ken Dodd
took out a policy on his trademark front teeth and Rod Stewart
insured his famous gravelly voice. Apparently, porn star John
Holmes had his… well, I expect you can guess.

Although I have taken out cover for damage to Derek the
Dolphin's fins and injury or accident to a guest involving a
vol-au-vent, personally, I like to take a chance or play the odds
when it comes to personal cover. You see, I'd take out insurance
on my life and then, with my luck, I'd probably live!

J

JAMS AND CREAM

When I was in the hotel business, I always insisted my staff followed my two basic rules in trying to give the best possible customer service. These were 'The answer is YES!' and 'Do it NOW!' The idea being that, if you said YES to a guest immediately, whatever the request and even if the answer was ultimately a no, it would make you try to find a solution, however difficult the demand. If you couldn't eventually discover a solution, at least the guest would know you tried your hardest to make it an actual YES! And, of course, 'do it NOW!' meant 'DO IT NOW!!!'

I remember once hearing some guests ask for a Devonshire Cream Tea and, to my horror, I heard a member of staff say, 'NO.' She told them that they couldn't have a cream tea because we'd run out of clotted cream. I was furious and jumped in, 'Of course you can have a cream tea. The answer is always "YES!" Please take a seat and we'll bring it straight over.'

I told the member of staff to start making the pot of tea and prepare the scones and strawberry jam while I quickly nipped out to buy some clotted cream. I jumped into my Bentley and sped off up the road. I knew of a shop not too far away that sold it. Should be simple to sort this out, I thought. Well, of course, it wasn't! Being the middle of summer, Torquay was heaving with cars and I got caught in a traffic jam. When I finally got to the shop, I couldn't find anywhere to park.

I drove around four times and by now was frantic trying to find a parking place. On the fifth attempt, I spotted a small space adjacent to the zebra crossing and managed to squeeze in on the end. My back wheel was just touching the end of the zigzag line but I thought, I'm only going to be a minute. It will be fine! I ran across the road and literally about sixty seconds later I was running back out of the shop clutching a big tub of clotted cream.

As I rushed back to my car, imagine my shock when I saw not one but TWO traffic wardens, who had, as if by magic, appeared from nowhere. I pretended they weren't there and strode past them before jumping into my car. As I started the engine, one of them knocked on my window. I called out that I was very sorry but I didn't have time for this sort of delay. I needed to get this back and I waved the large tub of clotted cream at him, which I thought would convince him of the urgency of my predicament!

I was about to put the Bentley into reverse when I noticed

the other traffic warden had moved and was now standing directly behind the car. I couldn't drive forward as I was almost touching the car in front as it was. 'Get out of the way!' I shouted. I started revving up the engine loudly, assuming he'd jump out of the way but he didn't! The other one shouted at me, 'If you don't turn off the engine, I'm going to call the police.' Unbelievable! These bloody traffic wardens were impossible. I had always assumed that they were some sort of police rejects and this just confirmed my view.

I knew that, if the police were called, I would be delayed even longer and, realising that I had no choice, I reluctantly wound down my window and switched off the engine. I couldn't really run over a traffic warden, no matter how bloody tempting, though I was sure no jury would convict me. But the trouble was that there was someone who had seen everything happen! A witness... the other traffic warden!

I then had to sit there for what seemed like an eternity while they not only had a right go at me but wrote me out a parking ticket – and not just any old parking ticket. A fine of £60 was bad enough but, because my back wheel was slightly over the zigzag line, I received three points on my licence as well... all for a tub of bloody clotted cream!

By the time I returned to the hotel, not only had the pot of tea gone cold but the guests had left, saying they couldn't wait any longer!

Un–bloody–believable!!!

JEHOVAH'S WITNESSES

I don't get many callers where I live now in the wilds of north London, which is the way I like it. I'm not one for cold callers, whether in person or on the phone. I'm not that fond of warm callers either, for that matter.

Someone once rang me up and asked me about an accident. Very nice of him. I said I couldn't remember it and he said I must be suffering from amnesia and would I like to claim some money. 'Of course,' I said but then I told him I couldn't remember my name and he rang off.

Of course, sometimes you don't realise that you're being door-stepped until you've been door-stepped and then it's too late to do anything about the door-steppers. But, occasionally, they find me; there are now all sorts of people that try it on – there's a mobile fishmonger from Newcastle who is always trying to sell me smoked haddock or something called 'hake'. He tells me it's fresh off the boat but then I notice he also sells tiger prawns with a label on the back that says 'Product of Thailand'. You can't tell me he caught that in the North Sea off Boulmer. I reckon he stops off at Tesco on the way, buys a load of fish and then passes it off as 'local produce'. Must be something to do with EU quotas.

I had a man wanting to build me a loft when I lived in a bungalow, a chap who said he just happened to be in the area and could repave my patio, which was a bit odd because I don't have a patio, and an attractive young woman trying to sell me her art – at least I think she said it was her art…

But, of course, the most famous interlopers are Jehovah's

Witnesses and they are very determined proselytisers. (Am I allowed to say that?) By the way, do you know why there are no Jehovah's Witnesses in heaven? Because God and Saint Peter hide behind the gates saying, 'Sssshhhhhh! Pretend we are not in!'

Anyway, a couple came round once and I thought they were selling me double glazing, so I felt sorry for them and let them in. Of course, once they were sitting in my lounge, they produced a copy of *The Watchtower* and told me I was doomed. I agreed with them but told them that was more to do with my ex-wives than God.

The bit I found really fascinating was that, apparently, Jehovah's Witnesses believe that, when the world ends, only 144,000 of them are actually going to be allowed to go to heaven, which must have been a bit of a bugger years ago when they first started out and were trying to recruit number 144,001 to the fold. Apparently, nowadays it's a bit like pyramid selling and, out of the millions of followers, only the first 144,000 people are actually guaranteed a place. Of course, in order to help increase numbers, periodically, they predict the end of the world; originally, it was set for 1914 and leading up to the date they had quite a few new followers join, although most of them left almost immediately afterwards – apparently, disappointed when the end of the world didn't happen. The same thing happened again in 1975 when the Armageddon prediction created a big influx of new followers, followed by a large number of disappointed leavers the next morning. Now, to play it safe, they say they aren't sure when the world will end so it's best to join ASAP so you don't miss out when it happens!

In the end, the Witnesses became frustrated by my lack of interest and the man asked me if I had any convictions and I replied, 'No, but I was once tempted to punch a Jehovah's Witness.' That soon got rid of them.

However, I do agree with them about not using profanity. There's no need for constant swearing, which shows a lack of imagination, although I do think the odd 'bloody' is OK in the right context.

Oh no, there's the doorbell. I'd better go. I just hope it's not another bloody Jehovah's Witness at the door.

K

KIDS

If I'm honest, I don't really like children… then again, if we're all honest, who bloody does? I think my dislike started when I was at school because the place was full of them! Not that I'm against kids. Well, not all of them anyway. I mean, I can put up with my own children, but I'm not exactly a lover of other people's children. Let's face it, who is?

The trouble is that there is now much overprotection and neurosis when it comes to looking after children. Kids these days are wrapped up in cotton wool. Literally. Well, obviously not literally… but you know what I mean.

There's a phrase 'helicopter parents', which describes parents who hover anxiously over their precious kids, paralysed by anxiety and fear of what could befall their little ones. Of course, we have to protect our children from obvious danger but now it's gone too far the other way.

We have now become far too protective towards children. In my day we used to roam around wartime bombsites amid unexploded bombs – apparently, that is no longer allowed, no doubt for some health-and-safety reason. But, whatever the reason, this is the sort of thing that makes playtime for kids much less interesting.

Apparently, playing conkers has been banned in school playgrounds for fear of grazed knuckles or even worse injuries. Climbing trees can only be considered under the guidance of a trained Sherpa, some kids have to be immunised against toxins before they can use crayons and I heard of one child forced to wear gauntlets and a helmet during a family game of Monopoly. (No doubt someone will insist on protective gear for bingo during my Party Nights.)

And what about those 'Child on Board' car stickers? Drives me mad! What are you supposed to do? Drive in a completely different way, play 'Puff the Magic Dragon' at top volume on your stereo and wave a teddy bear or a doll in their general direction? Unbelievable!

There are so many blogs, message boards and tweets about the right way to bring up your child. Could someone explain to me exactly what 'Mumsnet' is? I did try and Google it once but found myself on some very dodgy websites and immediately refreshed. There are vast numbers of parenting guides. When I was growing up, American childcare expert Dr Spock's books were all the rage – ridiculous that parents should take advice from a *Star Trek* character who wasn't even a real person. Illogical, I reckon.

There is also so much discussion about what women should or shouldn't do during pregnancy – despite my pro-smoking views, I certainly wouldn't recommend a female up the duff to draw on a Capstan. Drinking a glass of wine is considered OK but, apparently, not half a bottle of Captain Morgan. Moderation is the key word these days – quite contrary to how I've lived my life, of course.

Formula milk is considered 'poisonous' compared to breast-feeding. They say 'breast is best'. Well, I can't argue with that. Some of you may be surprised that I don't have a problem with a mother breastfeeding in public – as long as it is her own child and not some passing infant. Some men actually feel they are missing out that they are not able to breastfeed and wear a peculiar type of sling attached to some kind of breast pump so that they can bond with the baby and pretend they are performing the female role. Unbelievable!

There are, of course, also some frightening statistics about the best ways to nurture babies and the effect it will have later on in life when they're grown up. I heard somewhere that babies who share a bedroom with their parents are more likely to end up in Borstal aged sixteen, whereas babies who are left to cry themselves to sleep in their own cot often end up being Prime Minister. It's a complete minefield. I'm just glad I did it years ago and won't have to go through all that again.

Still, as that great songstress Whitney Houston once sang, 'I believe the children are our future.' And, of course, you can't actually argue with that sort of logic.

KILTS

One thing I've never understood is the whole idea of kilts.

Why, if you live in the most northerly part of the United Kingdom, would you want to wear a kilt instead of a decent pair of tweed or corduroy trousers?

I'm not against men in skirts on principle. Both Eddie Izzard and Grayson Perry can, in a certain light, look very fetching in little black numbers. There's also a long history of warriors and soldiers in skirts. Romans wore some sort of tunic, as did Anglo-Saxons and the Normans hundreds of years later. Zulu tribes in parts of Africa still wear skirts made of straw today, which makes sense when you think of the climate. But Scotland is bloody freezing in the winter.

The Scots could, of course, use that lovely thick tartan wool to knit a nice warm pair of trousers instead of wearing a kilt and letting the high winds blow just where you don't want them to! There is also the fact that 'True Scotsmen' aren't allowed to wear anything underneath. Apparently, in the forces it was the practice that the Sergeant Major would fix a mirror to a golf club, which he would then place near the feet of the soldiers to allow him to carry out a proper inspection on the parade ground... now, that's what you call inspecting your privates!

I have worn a kilt once, when I put on my special Scottish Night at the hotel, but that was in the middle of the summer in Sunny Torquay... and, before you ask, I'm not telling you! I did miss not having any pockets, although the sporran was really useful for containing my cigarettes and lighter.

There was a time, way back in 1746, when, to quell the Scottish clans and to stop an uprising, King George II actually banned the Scots from wearing kilts unless they were serving in the army. If you were up there in the Highlands and caught wearing a kilt, you could be punished by being sent to live abroad (in, most likely, a warm country) for seven years.

Blimey! If I'd been tramping through the Scottish glens and mountains wearing a kilt in the middle of winter in the freezing-cold weather, I'd be hoping to get bloody caught!

KINKY

I've got absolutely nothing to say on the subject – it's not that sort of book.

L

LEARNER DRIVERS

While stuck in traffic – which happens more and more these days – and having time to look around and take in the local views, I've noticed something interesting. Years ago, a learner driver would simply just display a red L-plate sign. That was that. You knew where you were (usually, directly behind them when they stalled time and time again). Now, once they've actually passed their test, new drivers display a green 'P' for Passed. I can only assume this is to warn other drivers that, despite having passed their driving tests and being let loose on the highways and byways, they really do not know what they are doing and remain a danger to other motorists.

Over the last few years, restaurants, hotels, greasy spoons – in fact, anywhere that has a kitchen to prepare food – have to display a rating, following an inspection by the Food Standards

Agency. The inspector takes in a number of factors, such as how hygienically the food is handled, prepared, cooked and stored, as well as the condition and cleanliness of the buildings.

The business is given one of six ratings. The top rating of 5 means that the business has 'very good' hygiene standards, whereas 'Ungraded' means the owners shouldn't even be looking at food, never mind cooking it or serving it to unsuspecting members of the public.

So my idea is that they should introduce something similar for drivers: a yearly examination where they test the competence of the driver, who would then have to display the result clearly and for all to see on their cars. In that way, other drivers would know immediately just how good or bad they are. Really terrible drivers would display an 'I' for Incompetent and, regardless of how they actually did on the test, all BMW drivers would just display a 'W' for... well, you know!

LETTUCE

It might surprise you to see that I have included lettuce here, especially as I don't eat anything green. But there is something about lettuce that's been bugging me. You see, many years ago I was actually a chef (well, not a proper chef, obviously, as my eating habits would have prevented me being some kind of Michel Roux Jr, Fanny Craddock or Gordon Ramsay – especially Gordon Ramsay as not only do I not cook like him, but I can't even swear like him).

Back then I was what they called a 'grill chef' in a fast-food type of restaurant called The Golden Egg, which was difficult as I hardly eat anything and so had no idea what I was serving up actually tasted like! Luckily, the menu was fairly simple and each item was cooked separately and then put on the plate: sausage, egg, chips and beans… that sort of thing. A combination of the lot was known as a 'GEM' in the trade, or a Golden Egg Mix to the customer.

And, let's face it, you'd hardly be expected to be able to test the taste and make sure it was cooked properly by dipping a bread and butter soldier in the egg before it went out to the table. You could easily tell if the beans were hot enough just by dipping your finger in them. I don't suppose you're allowed to do that now – what with the excesses of health and safety – but no one should have worried; I never burned my fingers.

There were a few other dishes on the menu, including omelettes. In fact, thinking about it, most of the dishes had an egg in there somewhere – I guess the clue was in the name of the restaurant! Of course, you won't be surprised to learn that eggs are another type of food that I don't eat. I mean, when did we start eating eggs anyway? How did it all begin? I can only assume that, one day, a long, long time ago, someone got fed up waiting for a chicken to hatch.

Although, of all our modern eating habits to have evolved, the strangest one, to me, has to be milk, although I have to admit that milk makes up my staple diet because I live on milky coffees or, to use the modern French phrase, lattes. But I want to know, how did it begin? Who was the first person to walk past a cow in a field, witness a baby calf suckling on its mother's udder and think to himself, 'I wouldn't mind some of that!' (Actually, I don't think we need to bother ourselves with answering that question.)

While breastfeeding babies is considered the most natural thing in the world, the thought of us adults drinking another human's milk horrifies us and yet, for some reason, we think it's fine to drink a similar substance produced by a different species – COWS!!!

Anyway, this section isn't about dairy produce, such as eggs or milk. In case you've forgotten, it's about LETTUCE – honestly! For those health-conscious customers who didn't fancy a fry-up, The Golden Egg did salads and, as the chef, I was responsible for ordering in all the ingredients to prepare these wonderful culinary delights. However, back then there were only two types of lettuce available – either crispy or floppy. I preferred the crispy one as it always looked less green than the floppy one… but, then again, I wasn't eating either of them!

Anyway, the whole point to this story is that just a few years ago I was asked to pick up a lettuce for someone from my local supermarket and expected to be met with a choice between crispy or floppy. But I soon discovered there was a whole aisle – in fact, as far as the eye could see – of hundreds of different types of lettuce with some strange names, such as the Blushed Butterhead (I thought that was a type of inflatable), the Curly Endive (named after a 1960s psychedelic group?) and the Iceberg.

I thought that to name a lettuce an Iceberg was a bit insensitive to the survivors of the *Titanic*; not that there are any survivors left anymore – they're all dead now – but I'm sure you can see what I'm driving at.

The question is: where did all these lettuces come from? And, more importantly, where were they all hiding before?!?

LETTUCE

LIBERTY, EQUALITY, PARKING

About fifteen years ago I visited France, for the first and last time, I might add. I'm not exactly a Francophile or lover of anything French for that matter – apart from Juliette Binoche, of course. Although, I have to say, if she smelt of garlic, it would put me right off and that would be the end of any possible romance. You see, *mes braves*, it's the eating habits of the French that horrify me.

I mean, why would any civilised country in the western world be proud of the fact that they eat FROGS LEGS and SNAILS? I know they invented the baguette, which actually doesn't taste bad with some nice ham in it, but that's before you learn that they only invented it – and, more importantly, made it that particular shape – so that the men could carry it around easily… by stuffing it down the inside of their trousers!

I only went to France because it was a special occasion – my then wife's fortieth birthday – so, as a romantic gesture, I decided to take her to Paris for the weekend. I had thought of taking her to Worthing but I spent a fortnight there one weekend and I didn't want to repeat that experience! Do you know that the seagulls fly upside down over Worthing because there's nothing worth messing on?

Anyway, Paris it was, and on the first day we were out walking and having a nose around, not far from the hotel that we were staying in. I didn't fancy driving in Paris, which is a bloody nightmare, being full of French drivers hooting, shouting and carrying on as if they owned the city. Apart from that, in France and other countries all around the world, the cars have the steering wheel and pedals on the passenger side, which means the passenger often ends up having to do all the driving!

To make matters worse, they also drive on the wrong side of the road and, if that wasn't bad enough, the roundabouts go round in the wrong direction. But the real killer, especially when you're driving in a different country and have no idea where you're going, is that all the signs are written in a foreign bloody language!

I know it's different nowadays because you can have a satnav, but I can't see how that could be any real help if you don't speak the language. I mean, by the time you've got out your phrase book and looked up and translated what the satnav voice is telling you to do, you'd have missed the bloody turning anyway!

So, anyhow, we found ourselves in a very posh part of Paris and decided to stop at one of the many pavement cafés and sit outside and enjoy a drink and a cigarette. Of course, we didn't have to sit outside, as this was before the dreaded smoking ban. Not that that seems to bother them in places like France anyway! (See 'C' for CAFÉS).

I was sitting admiring the view of a large building, which I assumed was the back of some art gallery or museum, as Paris seemed to be full of them, and I was also wondering how they could justify almost £8 for two tins of Coke (don't forget that this was also fifteen bloody years ago), when I noticed a large Mercedes pull up. To begin with, it seemed to double-park; then, without warning, the driver started to reverse between two parked cars.

I should explain that in Paris the parking tradition at the

time (probably still is) was to leave the car in neutral and the handbrake off so that cars could be moved. Here, there was only a tiny gap of about 4 ft – only just enough for either of the parked cars to pull out anyway. I stared in disbelief as I saw him gently bump into one of the cars but, unbelievably, he didn't stop and continued to reverse until he was pushing the car backwards, which then bumped into the car behind and so on, until a whole line of cars had been crammed into each other!

He'd actually made enough space for him to swing his wheel round and slowly started to edge forwards doing the same thing to the car in front of him. He bumped into this car as well, pushing it into the next one and the next one until the car parked at the very end had been pushed so far it was actually half blocking the adjoining road! He continued in this manner, going backwards and forwards several more times, until, eventually, he was parked neatly into a space that didn't exist before he came along. I've heard of creative parking but this was actually INCROYABLE!!!

M

MARRIAGES

Now, this is a subject I know a little about but I have to be careful what I say – especially with two ex-wives on the loose. You see, marriage isn't the most successful of institutions for me and I've always found it best to get married at midday – that way, if it doesn't work out, I haven't ruined the whole day.

After my experiences of being previously married, not once but twice (I'm one of the few people to have my divorce lawyer on speed dial), I'm beginning to think that these cultures that have arranged marriages might actually have the right idea. Let's face it – with forty per cent of marriages now ending in divorce in the UK, we're obviously rubbish at picking a partner. And, with my 100 per cent failure rate, I'm worse than most.

I reckon that, if a matchmaker had chosen a complete stranger for me to marry, I wouldn't be any worse off!

The alternative would be joining the Mormons when you can have a different wife for each day of the week. At least then, if you fall out with one, you've still got the other six to fall back on, if you see what I mean. The disadvantage is having seven mother-in-laws! And then, knowing my luck, the wives would all conspire to gang up on me. I'd probably end up with seven bloody divorces to pay for in one go.

In fact, that's the main reason I'm now single; since I lost all my money in the credit crunch, I'm now concentrating on rebuilding my wealth so that one day I can afford to get married again. Actually, now I think about it, it's not the cost of the wedding I'm saving up for – because you can actually do that bit fairly cheaply if you really want to. What I'm saving up for is the inevitable divorce – that's the bit that costs a bloody fortune!

MOBILE PHONES

Despite my phobias about technology (see 'M' for MANUAL FOR CHANGING LIGHT BULBS), I was actually one of the very first people to own a mobile phone. Honestly! It was a long time ago – in fact, it was such a long time ago that to make an emergency call I had to dial IX IX IX. Well, all right, it wasn't Roman times but it was about twenty-five years ago.

Those of you of a certain age will know that, when I say 'mobile', that's the one thing it wasn't. The phone was about the size of a suitcase (I think that's where the term 'trunk call' originated) and I pulled several muscles in places I didn't even know I had places just carrying it around, never mind trying to lift it up to my ear. Making a call on it was something else – very complicated and time-consuming – so I was all fingers and thumbs. In addition, each call cost a fortune – about £1.50 a minute, which in today's money would be about £5 a minute. So the end result was that I hardly ever made any calls. In fact, it was almost cheaper to get a taxi to someone's house and speak to them, rather than telephone them.

So, if there was a nearby telephone box, that's where I would walk to. Not only could I shelter from the elements but there was also a lot of reading material. No, not those pictures of ladies who seemed very fond of whips and leather. I'm talking about the directories, which seemed to be full of people I knew. But most of all, I found the shelf in the phone box a very useful place to rest my mobile while I put the money in the slot and made a call for 2p instead of spending the £1.50. That was fine, but the trouble was my mobile never rang… well, not when people realised it was going to cost them £1.50 a minute to phone me back.

I got rid of it after a few months, convinced that mobile phones were a daft idea and would never catch on! Of course, I've come around to thinking that mobiles can be useful and I am now thinking of buying a smartphone. The trouble is that it seems a bit of a nuisance to have to put on a suit every time I make a call.

N

NATURISTS AND NUDISTS

I'd always been a bit confused about the difference between someone who is a naturalist and someone who is a naturist. Well, that was until I was invited to a party once by one of the groups and turned up expecting to meet a load of David Attenborough types but was instead greeted by a load of completely naked people!

I had actually taken an ailing Aspidistra in the hope of finding a cure for my root rot but, once I realised that these were, indeed, naturists and not naturalists, I departed quickly, fully clothed! (My Aspidistra, however, never recovered.)

Sir David Attenborough made a wonderful television series called *The Frozen Planet* and, while I could never be considered a 'Green' type of person, I am, in principle, all for saving the planet and that type of thing. I mean, I'm not daft… because, if we do completely bugger up the earth to the point when it becomes uninhabitable, where are we all going to live?

Bearing in mind I'm one of the doubters who isn't really convinced that we've ever actually stepped foot on the moon (see 'U' for UFOs), I think it's highly unlikely that we'd somehow be able to transport all six billion of us to some other suitable planet trillions of light years away.

Although, it has to be said, I do have mixed feelings about all this global-warming stuff, especially when it was first mooted. If I'm honest, I was actually quite excited and looking forward to climate change – I was really quite tempted to throw all my fridges on the local rubbish dump and use up as many aerosols as quickly as I could!

This reaction was mainly because I am not keen on the cold – especially our winters – so the idea of not only enjoying lovely, long, hot summers but also milder and warmer winters really appealed to me. I thought it would be like suddenly finding we were living in some foreign country with a climate like Spain but without having to move. Perfect! (Or 'Perfecto!' as we then might be saying in Tunbridge Wells).

I knew that global warming meant that the ice caps would probably end up melting a bit and the sea levels would rise but, at the time, the hotels I owned were just off the main seafront and situated up a bit of a hill so, if the water levels rose and the seafront moved up a bit, I could find I had a prime position! It's not as if penguins and other wildlife wouldn't have anywhere to live – after all, the North and South Poles are huge and completely deserted, so they'd still have plenty of snow and ice to skate about on!

I didn't realise that what they actually predicted was that the seasons could become mixed up and the weather could become more extreme. We could have even more miserable cold days in the summer and, if we were lucky, just the odd few slightly warmer days in the winter. That's not much good – especially if you're planning a summer BBQ or something.

I know a lot of people work tirelessly trying to persuade governments around the world to change their ways and organise lots of events to raise awareness and I was actually witness to such a protest.

A few years ago I was in London at the same time as the naked bike ride happened to be taking place. The thinking behind the demonstration was to highlight society's 'oil dependency'. I would have thought that, if they really wanted to protest about that, they could have kept their clothes on and just got on a bus – apparently, that's the really 'Green' thing to do nowadays!

But, blimey, what a sight! Hundreds of them cycling through central London, and most were completely starkers. Half of them weren't even modest enough to sit down as they cycled along but, instead, actually stood up while they peddled (although, having seen how tiny the saddles are on some of these bikes nowadays, I'm not surprised!)

The thing that made me smile was that a few of them didn't even have their bikes with them – they were just running along the road naked. That isn't taking part in a naked bike ride – that's called streaking!

I'd like to make it clear here that I am no prude. I don't have a problem with people being bare if they really do want to hang out naked (if you see what I mean), for, as the saying goes, 'If we were meant to wear clothes, we'd have been born wearing them!' But they shouldn't flaunt it (if you see what I mean). There are lots of beaches that now allow that sort of thing – one of the main ones being in Brighton, although I have to say, it's hardly a beach – there isn't any proper sand. Have you noticed that nudist beaches are always rock or pebble ones and not nice, soft, sandy ones? That has always puzzled me. Then again, maybe it's obvious: that bloody sand can get everywhere!

But, to be honest, the most confusing bit about all this naturist and nudist stuff, and the bit I really don't understand, is that the public it seems to attract – those naturist enthusiasts; the people who like to get naked in public – are actually the very ones that should be made to keep all their clothes on.

NIGHTMARES (OR, IF YOU PREFER, BLOODY NIGHTMARES)

One thing I do know, as sure as eggs are eggs (what a ridiculous expression! What does it mean? I wish I'd never used it now…), I've had a few disasters over the years.

As you probably realise by now, life hasn't always run smoothly for me! Over the years, I've established and run a string of businesses and have made and lost a fortune along the way.

I started my very first business aged just nineteen when I decided I was going to start selling video recorders door to door. It seemed like a brilliant idea because at the time video recorders were a brand-new concept and most people had never actually seen one, never mind knew what they could do. So my concept was to take them round to people's homes, give them a demonstration and then sell them a machine. It seemed like the perfect plan.

You'll notice I used the word 'seemed'. You see, the business didn't do quite as well as it should have done. The trouble was that, at that time in the 1970s, there were lots of problems importing enough recorders from China. Wholesalers found that supplies were sometimes scarce and very hard to get hold of. However, I decided I wasn't going to miss out on this great opportunity and would spend what it took to make this business a success. I had an opportunity to buy a big job-lot of recorders and stocked up with over a hundred of them, thereby getting myself into a huge amount of debt. There were two systems – VHS and Betamax – and I chose… yes, you've guessed it…

BETAMAX, which lost out in the format war to VHS and became obsolete almost immediately. I lost all my money.

As Entertainment Manager, I've had my fair share of trouble when I've come up with brilliant schemes to bring in the punters but I was sometimes thwarted by bad luck. I tried to put on a 'Wrestling Spectacular' – only to have to cancel the show when I discovered you needed a special licence to hold 'fighting' on your premises. Who knew wrestling was fighting and not entertainment? The wrestlers weren't too happy and some of them were huge. Bloody Nightmare.

And who could predict that my idea for a family fun day would be ruined by a hurricane? In Torquay of all places and a hurricane called BERTHA at that! I wonder why they name hurricanes after women. It's a good job I'm not a chauvinist – otherwise I'd have some very likely explanations.

Of course, that really wasn't my fault. I am naturally unlucky and, of course, when something goes wrong, the situation often develops from a minor irritation to a serious setback and then into a complete bloody disaster! With my luck, if I broke a mirror, I'd probably get twenty-one years' bad luck! Even when things seem to go right and I'm making a success of an event, it tends to turn into a bloody nightmare. If I did manage to put Torquay on the map and were given the keys to the city, knowing me, I'd probably lock myself out. (Yes, I know Torquay isn't a city – it's a town – but you can't be given the keys to a town, so the gag wouldn't work.)

I know I'm also a nightmare to live with. I've been told many times in no uncertain terms, and it's about the only thing my ex-wives and I agreed on. There were times when it seemed everything I touched went wrong.

But, having said that, perhaps all this bad luck is really just my own fault. Maybe I'm just not superstitious enough and bring it on myself. Some things do make sense to me – in my hotels I always occupied room 12a instead of 13, and I can see why it might be unlucky to walk under a ladder. But what I really fail to understand is why a bird messing on you is considered lucky! Apparently, it comes from the belief that the likelihood of it happening is about a million to one so, if you're lucky enough to be covered in bird's mess, you also just might be lucky enough to win the lottery!

I don't believe a word of it. I've been messed on three times in my life by birds and I've never once won the bloody lottery.

Absolute Nightmare!!!

O

OPTIMISM

When it comes to considering whether the glass is half-full or half-empty, I've always thought that the glass is actually overflowing – even when it's not. And, at the risk of sounding like Nellie in *South Pacific*, 'I am a cockeyed optimist.' It's true. In fact, OPTIMISM is my middle name. Well, it isn't… it's actually Lawrence, but it's been said by many wise folk that I'm the man who put the 'O' in Optimism. I'm very flattered, of course, but it doesn't really make sense. For a start, I've never heard of 'Ptimism' so the 'O' must have always been there!

The celebrated Monty Python song, 'Always Look on the Bright Side of Life' sums it up for me and is one of my favourite songs, along with 'When You're Smiling', which was my dad's old signature tune.

Someone once said that the optimist invented the airplane and the pessimist the parachute! Well, I've always been an optimist and looked for the positive in everything – quite the opposite of pessimists, who see the worst side of everything and tend to live by such mottos such as:

> *'When one door closes, another one slams in your face!'*
> *'Every cloud has a dark-grey lining!'*
> *'Life is full of downs and downs!'*

Of course, the one good thing about being a miserable bugger is you're never really going to be disappointed. In fact, when something does go right, it will come as a massive surprise, whereas being an optimist means you spend half your life being disappointed when things don't quite turn out as you expected!

But, as an optimist, you see each failure and disappointment as an opportunity to explore something new! You see, no matter what disaster I've had to face throughout my life – and there've been more than a few – I've always remained positive and faced it with humour and a smile because, as the old adage goes, 'It's no use crying over spilt milk.' You can't undo what's done, so why get upset about it?

Although, I have to say, if all the shops were shut and I'd just spilled the last drop of milk, which meant I'd run out and couldn't have a milky coffee first thing in the morning, it might be a different story!

OPTIMISM

In which case, my motto might be, 'The light at the end of the tunnel might be another train…'

P

PANTOMIME

Oh yes, it is!

I was rather surprised to be offered the part of the King in *Sleeping Beauty* at Torquay's Princess Theatre, but then I thought, if Frank Bruno, Gok Wan and Ann Widdecombe could tread the festive boards, there was no reason why I couldn't appear in a Christmas panto.

I had assumed that the part would be played by a better-known personality – a proper star, or at least someone larger – but, when the script arrived, it became obvious that in the previous year the King had, in fact, been played by comedian Syd LITTLE! I quickly realised that I had only got the role because the costume fitted me and I also soon realised that the current script – the one I had to learn – had been written especially for him.

In fact, it was pretty obvious from my opening line, which read, 'Hands up those of you who thought I was dead!' This was supposedly based on the fact that Syd is in his late seventies and people may not have known if he was still alive or not. I have to say that, if I had been in the audience then, I might well have put my hand up!

Anyway, I took my part very seriously – after all, panto is no laughing matter. In fact, I've been to some shows that were so terrible that they should have given you your money back on the way in. I took great care in learning my lines, which I was really worried about, as I have a terrible memory. It was all a bit of a trial – at one stage I put the script down and couldn't remember where I'd put it.

I was, naturally, a bit nervous on opening night, as I'd never done this sort of thing in public before – certainly not without inflatables – but I soon settled into the role and very much enjoyed playing 'King Egbert the Oval'. I had to sing, of course, and, actually, I haven't got a bad voice, although it would be unfair to compare my voice to Frank Sinatra's – he can't really defend himself now.

I'd like to do some more panto. I see myself more as Buttons than the back end of a horse – I saw enough of those when I was a professional tipster. No, Buttons is a very sympathetic character and me all over. Definite typecasting. By the way, do you know why Cinderella wasn't very good at football? Because she had a pumpkin as a coach.

But what I'd really love is to do some serious acting. Not become a movie star but perhaps a character actor. More of a

Laurence Olivier than a Robert De Niro. I reckon I could play Hamlet, Romeo… even King Lear. I've always liked that line of his, 'Out vile jelly, where is thy lustre now?' (I actually quite like jelly, although it doesn't compare with my love of blancmange.)

Or there is the 'Scottish Play' – you see I'm already behaving like a true thespian and avoiding mentioning *Macbeth*, which is apparently bad luck. Thank goodness I'm not superstitious… touch wood.

PEOPLE

Someone once said (actually, they sang), 'People who need people are the luckiest people in the world.' No, I don't understand what that means either, but, for some reason, it became a very famous song and sold a lot of copies.

As far as I'm concerned, there are three types of people: Rich, Poor and, of course, Normal. If I'm honest, normal people are by far my favourite, although I'm not sure it's the category that most people would put me in! And, financially, I'd be lying if I said I didn't want to be rich again. And if they're honest, most people would rather be rich than normal. And they would certainly rather be rich than poor. That doesn't mean they all want to behave like rich people – they just want more money!

Normal people are by far the best people… not too poor and not too rich, just… well… normal.

Now, poor people are a different breed altogether – through no fault of their own, they tell me. Apparently, 'poor' is another one of those four-letter words that you're not meant to say. While I was doing my Party Night Tour, I sold the tickets in three different price brackets: VIP Tickets for rich people, Normal Tickets for normal, hardworking people and some special cheap tickets at half the price of the VIP ones, especially for poor people.

On my Facebook page I posted a picture of the hotel in Liverpool where one of the Party Nights was to be held and it looked very posh. I made the comment that, 'I hoped they let the "Poor" people in.' Well, this woman 'unfriended' me and stated that she was going to report me for saying such a terrible thing and using the term 'Poor' people'! I don't know to whom or where she was going to report me – the 'Poor People Police', I suppose.

Anyway, my reply was that I was very fond of poor people, in my own way, and that, if I really didn't like them, I'd hardly have offered them cheap tickets to come to one of my Party Nights!

Of course, as in many of my best-laid schemes, it didn't quite go to plan, as I discovered that some of the rich people were too tight to pay for VIP tickets and ended up buying Poor People Tickets, which were half the price. No doubt, this sort of underhand wheeling and dealing is probably how they became rich in the first place. And to make it worse, some poor people saved up and purchased the expensive VIP tickets, so the whole thing became a bloody nightmare!

Some of my best friends are poor people, although I'd prefer it if some of my best friends were rich people! No, I don't have anything against poor people. In fact, there have been quite a few times in my life when I was actually one of them. When you owe more than your net worth, even the homeless person with all his belongings stuffed in a carrier bag is richer then you are! If I'm honest, I didn't really enjoy being a poor person and I've never been what could be described as normal. I've either been rich or poor and believe me, while I know money can't buy you happiness, it can pay the bloody bills!

POLITICS

The trouble with democracy is that it doesn't work. You only have to look at the state of the country to know that. The problem is that half the time the people who put themselves up for election are the last people you want in power. Ultimately, their only goal is to try to be seen to make less cock-ups than the last lot in the hope they'll be given the job for another five years.

They should introduce a special kind of proportional representation so the MPs directly reflect the people they represent; so that, if fifty per cent of the population earn £20,000 a year or less, they should make up fifty per cent of the government. In the same way, six per cent unemployed and those on 'zero contracts' (probably about seventy-five per cent these days) could constitute the numbers in the House of Commons. We could also end up with five per cent single parents, ten per cent Polish builders, two per cent trainspotters, one per cent aliens (see 'U' for UFOs) and maybe even the odd politician!

Failing that, of course, I could put myself up for election as a sort of benign dictator in the guise of Prime Minister. There is a lot I could do to make the country a better place to live. Better still, why don't *you* make a list of six things you'd like to ban or laws you'd like to introduce, tweet them to me at @_MarkJenkins and I'll reward the best ideas in the style of 'Manager Mark', with an invitation to one of my 'Party Nights'. ★★★

★★★Oh... apparently the editor and my agent have put an end to that idea. Might crash the whole information superhighway, apparently.

But if you've got nothing better to do, make the list anyway.

1...
2...
3...
4...
5...
6...

PUBLIC HOLIDAYS

These are also known as bank holidays but, in recent years, it would seem that some of the banks have now started to open on bank holidays, so it seems a bit daft to continue to call them bank holidays when the only places that aren't having a holiday are the banks!

One thing that has always bothered me is that we don't have a holiday to celebrate our own patron saint, St George. St Patrick's Day in Ireland has become a world-renowned holiday and is actually celebrated more in England than St George's

Day is, although I suspect that has more to do with Guinness than deference to shamrocks and saints!

I wouldn't mind but all St Patrick did was to rid Ireland of a few snakes, which then ended up living all over the rest of the world. I call that an early example of Nimbyism! It's all very well clearing your own backyard of all those reptiles, but I bet India or Africa weren't best pleased at having to cope with the pythons and cobras that were ousted from the Emerald Isle.

It was very different with St George. You see, he actually disposed of all dragons in England, which at the time were a tremendous threat to everyone from Budleigh Salterton to Robin Hood's Bay. He was actually 100 per cent successful in his firefighting – not only in Blighty but all over the world. And we know that because not one single person reading this will ever have seen a dragon in real life anywhere across the globe. That is incontrovertible proof!

Of course, there are those professional doubters and sceptical types who claim dragons were only mythical creatures and that St George was actually just some Greek bloke serving in the Roman army. In any case, I reckon the fact that he had probably never heard of England let alone visited our sunny shores here shouldn't stop us having St George's Day as a public holiday.

The Scots have a public holiday on St Andrew's Day, wear kilts, eat haggis, drink malt whisky and even eat deep-fried Mars bars, Northern Ireland has St Patrick's Day as a holiday and there are some Welsh people I know who take time off on St David's Day to watch rugby while singing selections from the Harry Secombe songbook.

I do think it's time that 23 April (St George's Day) is adopted as a bank holiday but, of course, the other option is for us to have a brand-new patron saint and have their birthday as a special public holiday. I would suggest someone who is much loved and held in high regard by everyone in England. A folk hero or a national treasure, if you will.

29 March happens to be my birthday, if anyone is interested…

PUBLIC TRANSPORT

I'm not very keen on public transport as I prefer to drive to places (see 'C' for CARS), but sometimes you don't have a choice. I remember the first time I had to attend an important meeting in the centre of London and, what with congestion charge and parking fees, I decided to live dangerously and entrust my life to London Transport.

I purchased an Oyster Card (that's the only time I've ever spent money on anything to do with oysters), went to my local underground station and, with some trepidation, boarded a tube train. I had to change twice, which was a bloody nightmare because that underground map is unfathomable, especially if you're colour blind. (Luckily I'm not colour blind but I still can't work it out.)

I was worried that, when I reached the underground station nearest to my destination, I might get lost, as I usually do. So I came up with a cunning plan: I took with me my satnav from the car. I'd already pre-programmed the postcode for when I arrived. Brilliant, eh? Simple, I thought. All I have to do is walk along the pavements as directed by the satnav.

The trouble – and what I didn't think of – was that the satnav wouldn't let me walk the wrong way down the one-way streets; I had to follow all the one-way directions and all the diversions for road works and the like. And believe me, London's full of them. I'm surprised it didn't make me avoid the speed bumps, which are everywhere too! The bloody satnav took me all round the houses – literally – so I had to walk twice as far and it took me twice as long. Hours, in fact.

I'd have probably got there quicker if I had got lost! Next time I have to go to a meeting in the middle of London I'm going to buy a bloody map – not that I'll understand it, of course!

Incidentally, the satnav in the Bentley (see 'C' for CARS) used to take me via 5-star hotels, Michelin-starred restaurants and country clubs but my new, cheap satnav takes me via Travelodges, McDonalds and Wetherspoons!

Q

THE QUEEN

One of the things that I believe makes this country such a unique and great place to live compared with anywhere else in the world is our wonderful royal family. Well, not all of them, obviously – a few of them aren't as great as they should be. I've never known what Prince Andrew does for a living and he does have some dodgy business friends, although Koo Stark must go down as one of his successful mergers.

Prince Philip is also prone to the odd gaffe – quite a number, actually – such as when he asked a sea cadet if she was a stripper, describing the Duke Of York's house (see above) as 'a tart's bedroom' and asking the Cayman islanders if they were descended from pirates, as well as even worse things that I'm not going to mention for fear of upsetting the Palace.

But the good old Queen has certainly never let us down and she never will. Yes, I'm a royalist and proud of it. I don't think I would ever be fazed by meeting most anyone. If I'm honest, there isn't a prime minster or president or, indeed, anyone from the world of show business that would intimidate me. No, there is only one person on this entire planet that I would be somewhat nervous about meeting and that would be the Queen. I would just have to hope that she approved of *The Hotel*. Actually, I'm sure Her Majesty watched the show. You know, I think I missed a trick there – I could have asked her to come down and cut a ribbon for one of my events or call the start of the Inflatable Dolphin Racing. I'm sure she would have loved that.

But I would still have been nervous in her presence. Did you know that the death penalty was still in place right up until 1998 for anyone who actually harmed the Queen or even plotted that sort of thing? Not that I would, of course, but accidents do happen. Supposing she got hit on the head by an errant Derek the Dolphin, or a member of my staff bumped into her by mistake and sent her headlong into the pool? I could have ended up in the Tower... headless.

There was even a time when the death penalty could be applied if you killed one of her swans. Yes! For killing a swan, you could actually be tried for treason! That really shocked me... For killing a corgi, I could understand... but swans...

Apparently, the Queen owns ALL of them – swans, not corgis. She's actually down to just two of those. In fact, she's recently announced that, now she's reached the grand old age of eighty-nine, she won't be replacing them anymore in case she trips over one and hurts herself. Maybe she could switch to a St Bernard – a breed so large that not only would she not trip over one but, if she did have a fall, she could have a quick swig of brandy to help calm her. That's definitely what her sister, Princess Margaret, would have done, as long as the dog was carrying a gin and tonic and not the usual brandy!

Now, where was I? Oh yes, swans! The Queen used to own them ALL but now, apparently, she just owns the 'mute' ones. That makes sense because those swans can be a noisy lot – so I guess it's better to only have the ones that don't make any noise! (Even so, that's still a lot of bloody swans. I bet her bread bill is huge...)

Of course, it's absolutely right and correct that in a democracy people have free speech and all her subjects are entitled to their opinion. Well, there are people who dare to say we'd be better off without the royal family. They are, of course, entitled to their opinion. But, in my opinion, I call that treason and I've only got one thing to say to it: 'Off with their heads!'

QUESTIONS (AND ANSWERS)

As we're now on the letter 'Q', I'm sure you've noticed I have quite an inQuisitive mind and I hate it when I don't know the answer to something. Now, I did think that I could use this bit to pose some questions, hoping that some of you might be able to answer them for me. Questions that have always intrigued me, such as 'Why is it that the time of day when the traffic is at its slowest is called "Rush Hour"?', 'What if the "Hokey Cokey"really is what it's all about?', 'Why doesn't Tarzan have a beard?', 'Why don't you ever see the headline, PSYCHIC WINS LOTTERY?' and 'What was the best thing before sliced bread?'

But then I thought, what's the point? Even if you answer them, how will I know your answers? I mean, it's not like an exam where I'm going to be going round collecting the books when you've finished with them (unless you all decide to return the books and demand a refund. Well, I'm afraid it's too late for that – you've made it to 'Q' and so the bloody book is second-hand now. If you weren't satisfied with the content, you should have said something before and now I'm afraid it's now too late to get your money back!)

Anyway, I've always wanted to be the subject of one of those Q&A interviews that you see in most magazines. Unfortunately, as no one has actually asked me, I thought I'd complete one by both asking myself the questions and then answering them. To keep it simple, I've decided all the questions will be about me, then, hopefully, I'll know the answers. Here we go…

So, Manager Mark, were you naughty as a child?

Oh that's a tricky one to start with… I actually spent half my school life either in detention or standing outside the headmaster's office being in trouble for doing something wrong. I found certain textbooks quite useful, especially the slightly thicker ones, mainly because I'd end up sticking them down the back of my trousers so the bloody cane didn't sting so much.

One of my tricks was to set all the fire alarms off, which meant we all had to go outside and spend the next hour or so standing around in the middle of the sports field while they took a register of the whole school. That way, I'd end up missing the whole of the next lesson, which was perfect if I knew I was going to be in big trouble for not doing my homework. (I didn't believe in homework!) It was a brilliant plan until one day when I set the alarm off and hadn't noticed that it was pouring down with bloody rain outside and we all got soaked.

What really is your worst nightmare?

I have a recurring dream that I am being suffocated by a huge marshmallow. When I wake up, my pillow is always missing.

What is your first showbiz memory?

I'm glad you asked me that, Mark. When I was four, my dad entered me into my first talent contest at a Butlins holiday camp. My act was mainly singing and telling a few gags but I also played a plastic toy trumpet. Unfortunately, they decided to put me on last and I got so bored while I was backstage waiting that I sat there chewing the mouthpiece of the trumpet. By the time I went on stage, I'd chewed it so much that I couldn't get a bloody sound of it! But I still came first in the competition and won a week's free holiday. In fact, I never claimed the prize and I've still got the certificate… I wonder if it's too late to contact Butlins. I could do with a free holiday!

What's your favourite smell?
The aroma of a King Size Dunhill. I love the smell of tobacco in the morning.

And your favourite food?
That's a daft question, if you don't mind me saying. You should know by now that I'm not really a lover of food. In fact, eating in general is a bit of a chore to the point that some days I have to remind myself to do it!

When I was little and people were first talking about going into space, I assumed that, by the time I was older, we wouldn't bother with all this normal type of food anymore and that, to help stop starvation around the world in the future, we'd all be eating the same sort of stuff the spacemen did, with everything coming out of a tube like toothpaste. In fact, I was really looking forward to it. Of course, knowing my luck, they'd make it taste of spinach.

When did you last have sex?
I'm sorry, Mark, but that's really none of your business. I can't believe you asked me that! But I will divulge that it was my father who told me about the birds and the bees. Although he

never did get around to the bees – I was too shocked when he told me about the birds.

What's your favourite word?
Aardvark. I saw one in a zzoo once.

Who is the most famous celebrity you've met?
I've been fortunate enough to meet some amazing people, including some of our top celebrities and, while appearing as a guest on various shows, I've even been on TV with quite a few of them.

A few months ago I was in the centre of London with my manager on my way to see a TV production company about an idea they had for me for a new TV show. As we were walking along the road, this very smartly dressed, attractive lady came up to me and said, 'Oh, it's you… I'm you're biggest fan!' At which point my manager piped up and said to the lady, 'I'm actually YOUR biggest fan!' I thought this was a rather odd thing to say to a complete stranger but I ignored her and continued my chat with the lady.

I was about to start my Party Night Tour and, not one to miss an opportunity, as this woman claimed to be 'my biggest fan', I thought I might be able to flog her a few tickets – VIP, of course. I could see she wasn't a normal person and certainly not a poor person. She informed me that she spent most of her time in America, so wouldn't be here on those particular dates but wished me well with the tour. I was rather upset that I hadn't managed to flog her any tickets but, as we walked away, my manager said, 'Do you know who that was?'

'No idea,' I said.

'That,' my manager said with complete disbelief, 'was... Tracey Ullman!'

She's a huge star in America but I hadn't recognised her. Unbelievable!!!

(Please don't repeat this story if you also bump into her somewhere.)

What is the closest you've come to dying?

I've luckily avoided any serious illness or accidents but I nearly 'died a death' at my Party Night in Cricklewood.

What is your most treasured possession?

Derek the Dolphin (see 'I' for INFLATABLES).

What's the one thing that would most improve your quality of life?

Come on, Mark, you must know the answer to this! I've always had a passion for Bentleys. In fact, when I was fourteen, I made a vow to myself that, by the time I was fifty, I'd somehow own one. I achieved my lifelong dream five years ahead of schedule but then, thanks to the credit crunch six years later, I was forced to sell the Bentley. (I did replace it for a while but it wasn't really mine – it was on credit – and in the end I had to let that one go as well!) My dream now is to get my Bentley back, although it took thirty years of hard work to get the first one and so, if it takes another thirty years, by the time I do get it, I'll be eight-five and too old to bloody drive!

Who or what is the greatest love of your life?

That's easy. My mum, of course!

R

RATINGS

These days there are all sorts of ratings on various services or businesses. You can have television ratings in terms of viewing figures, healthcare provider ratings (which presumably include things like the survival rate of patients undergoing veruca operations in hospital corridors) and, of course, credit ratings, which I have always tried to avoid. Enlisted members of the navy are also called ratings – so presumably, if they are judged by their performance, that must be termed as 'ratings ratings' (I'm not including apostrophe's here as it's a spelling nightmare and I don't want to be rated on my grammar).

But this is just a way of introducing my next topic and the type of rating that has affected my life the most. You see, it's always amused me that hotels and some restaurants are still rated by motoring organizations. I could never really understand how two companies specialising in supplying mobile car mechanics became such experts on hotels!

Let me explain. For years all the star ratings were given out by either the RAC or the AA, and many hotels used to pay both of these organizations for such reviews… including me! The AA and RAC used to charge me about £500 a year to send a critic undercover, who would then stay the night in secret and the following morning make themselves known to me. In a 'big reveal', they would then tell me how many stars I had or hadn't got and provide me with me a lengthy list of everything that they thought was wrong!

I did this for a while until one year I decided I'd be better off saving myself the £500 and using the money to put right some of the things they were no doubt going to moan about. Let's face it, when it came to knowing what was wrong with my hotel, I knew much better than them! And what's more, I could then award my hotels three stars anyway!

It became even more confusing recently when 'the powers that be' did away with the notion of 'diamonds' for guesthouses and gave them stars as well. Unbelievable! There's a big bloody difference between the service offered and expected by a so-called 5-star, tiny, three-bedroom guesthouse and a proper 5-star hotel.

Of course, really posh restaurants can also be rated by the AA and awarded special 'rosettes' if the food critics are served with all this modern-type food – 'nouvelle cuisine' – the kind that looks like a sample (albeit a very pretty one) on the plate, despite the fact that they actually charge you double the amount for half the quantity!

But the one that really gets me is that the so called 'crème-de-la crème' – the very top restaurants in the world – are the ones that are, in fact, rated and awarded special stars by a TYRE company! I can only assume the logo of the Michelin Man is some kind of proof that they have, in fact, eaten in every bloody top restaurant in the world!

RELIGION

Let me begin by saying I'm not really a fan of religion – any religion, that is. So if you hold strong religious convictions, maybe you should skip this bit! Don't get me wrong: it must be really comforting to have a faith, a source of belief and a support system. In fact, in many ways, I sort of envy those that do. And not just for when you're alive but also for when you pop your clogs.

You see, I believe that, when you die, that's it... that's the end. There's just nothing. I think I'm just going to become worm food! It must be quite handy to have some trust in the afterlife and reincarnation, although, if you're a Buddhist, I understand that karma can play a transcendental trick on you by bringing you back as a cockroach or Jeremy Kyle. I wouldn't like that – especially being Jeremy Kyle.

But I suppose you religious lot do at least have something to look forward to, rather than just 'The Long Goodbye', although, if you're one of those really fundamentalist ISIS-types, I'm not sure how having seventy-two virgins waiting for you is going to do you any favours if you've blown yourself into a thousand pieces at the time of martyrdom!

Other religions do offer a different outcome. Apparently, if you've been really naughty, you're likely to end up burning for eternity in hell, which can't be much to look forward to. And, of course, if you're good, you don't get the virgins but you do get to sit around all day on the clouds playing harps and being bothered by angels and cherubs.

I can sort of understand the concept, but I've always found

religion to be the most confusing of subjects, mainly because there is so much choice. (One thing that bothers me about all the faiths is that not one of them ever mentions dinosaurs.) Apparently, there are hundreds of religions, although, from what I understand, they are grouped into five main ones.

In order to be religious you have to believe in the notion that there is some sort of superior being looking down on us who is responsible for everything. I find that difficult to believe because even Alan Sugar doesn't have that kind of omnipresent power (although Richard Branson does). And, of course, the reason the world is such a terrible place, with constant wars, disasters and strife, is that all of these gods have given us freewill to do whatever we want – including killing each other in the name of religion.

If it was up to me, I'd like to see all the actual gods from all the different religions compete in some sort of reality-telly show. How about an *X Factor*-type talent contest where all the gods perform and 'the winner takes all'? (My money would be on Buddha, who I understand was quite a hoofer.) So, if we have to have religion on this planet, we will end up with just one god and one belief system and then there really would be peace on earth and goodwill to all men. Amen.

5

SALES AND MARKETING

I have spent half my life in sales – that's working in them, not going to them – and I'm going to let you into a little secret: most sales are a bit of a con! In lots of cases, the so-called sale price is actually the real price and it's just a way of persuading you to buy something by making you think you're getting a bargain! And who can resist a bargain?!

It means you're saving money, although, of course, you'd save even more money if you didn't buy the item in the first place – or even in the second place. I think the furniture retailers DFS have had a sale on their sofas since they first started trading! To get around advertising laws, many other shops put some of their items in the corner of their least popular outlet with an overinflated price, just so they can prove it really is on sale by stating it was previously displayed at the higher price. Of course, nobody bought it at that higher price – why would they? It was hidden in the corner with a price tag asking for twice what it's really probably worth!

There was a time in advertising when you had to prove that what you were claiming in your ad was actually true! Imagine that! I can remember years ago seeing an advert on TV in which a man advertising some glue had his clothes stuck to a big hoarding while a helicopter lifted the board hundreds of feet into the air. Miraculously, he didn't fall off… or, if he did, they didn't show it! I didn't actually need the glue but I was convinced enough to buy some, thinking I could use it to hang my wallpaper!

Nowadays it seems the ad men and women can get away with ridiculous claims. I recently bought a torch and on the box it proudly stated that it had the power of one million candles! As if anybody actually needs the same amount of light that one million candles can produce! I didn't actually go into the shop thinking, 'Mmm… the place I'm going to use this torch is going to be really dark. What I really need is a huge number of candles. Yes, that would be much better. Now, I wonder how many candles I might need instead of a torch. Erm… let me think… I know – I think about a million candles would probably give me just enough light.' And then I'd read the blurb on the torch's packaging and be delighted that I didn't need to buy the candles after all – this very torch is perfect!'

Unbelievable!!!

And in any case, how do they know that the light shining from the torch is the equivalent of one million candles? Did they really test it? And how? I had visions of a giant warehouse with a million candles all stood up waiting for some poor soul – perhaps an out-of-work lamplighter or a frustrated pyromaniac – whose job it was to light all the candles. Surely by the time you've lit candle number 768,793 the first one would have burned out and you'd have to start again.

I don't believe a bloody word of it!

The trouble is we're all victims of marketing and even I – with all my experience in this world – fall prey to such merchandising. You see, I actually bought two torches! Well, you never know when you might need the power of two million candles.

SAUSAGES

They say you can't judge a book by its cover but I believe you can judge a person by their sausage. From my time in the hotel business, I discovered that posh people are a fussy lot when it comes to sausages: not only do they expect them to be bigger but they like to know if they've won any awards! Can you imagine? And it doesn't stop there – sausage snobs want to know where they come from and get very excited if they discover them to be 'local produce'. They need to know how far their sausage has travelled and probably by which mode of transport. (Petrol fumes can apparently affect the chemical balance within the skin.) And that's another thing: the sausage makers stuff the sausages with all sorts of offal, bread and even water to plump them out and dye them to make them look like sausage-coloured sausages.

The humble banger is one of the great British traditions and, buried in a giant Yorkshire pudding, is one of my favourite dishes – although quite why it's called toad in the hole is beyond me. As far as I'm aware, toads have never been made into sausages. Maybe the dish originated in France and, knowing their love of frogs' legs, etc. over there, they use actual toads instead of sausages.

There are now over 400 varieties available in the UK alone and they come in many shapes and names worldwide: frankfurter (Germany), klobás (Czech Republic), chorizo (Spain), andouillette (France), and the noble chipolata (Scarborough). Anyway, you get the message and I'll stop there before this turns into the Eurovision Sausage Contest.

The word 'sausage' can also be used as a term of endearment – for example, 'You look lovely tonight, my little sausage,' or, 'Oh, you *are* funny, my silly sausage.' I must warn you, however, not to use such a phrase to vegetarians, who I understand are often much insulted by this expression of affection and would prefer to be addressed as 'My precious little turnip.'

Of course, the sausage is often used as a source of humour and is an obvious euphemism. But I'm not going there. I hate double entendres so I'll leave it out.

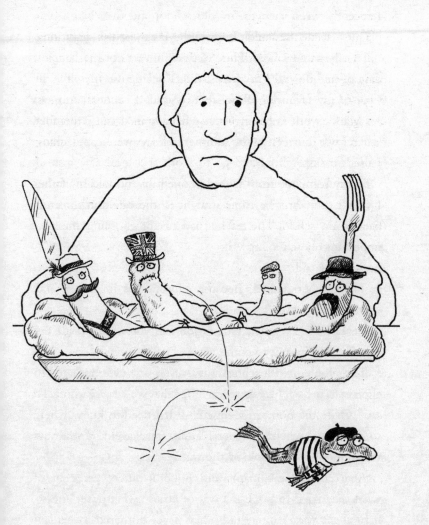

SCHOOL

I recently went back to my old school and they had a blue plaque outside the building – it said: MARK JENKINS SLEPT HERE.

I really hated school. They were definitely not the happiest days of my life and I'm afraid I didn't distinguish myself at all. One of my favourite school reports read, 'I cannot comment on Mark's work as he's never handed any in.' I can remember, when I was fourteen, as the summer holidays were approaching, I used to skip school and go to work at a local café instead. One day, someone from school phoned up and told my father I wasn't there and he came straight to the café and took me back to my school. The teacher had a right go, telling me how important my schooling was:

'Why?' I said.

The teacher replied, 'Because education is important and, without it, you won't get a job.'

I told him, 'I've got a bloody job and you've just made my dad drag me from it to come here!'

The problem with school was that no one ever bothered to explain to me why we were learning what we were learning. I'd say, 'What's the point in Geography? If I need to know where somewhere is when I'm older, I'll ask a travel agent.' (I've always sworn by Thomas Cook, by the way.)

Apart from basic maths and English, ninety per cent of what they tried to teach me was of no use whatsoever and so, naturally, I wasn't interested. They never bothered to explain that it's not what you learn but the fact that, by passing a few exams in different subjects, you can show a future employer that you are capable of learning something. I can't see the point... Just teach kids the stuff that you need to know and test them on that instead.

Of course, nowadays you don't have to bother with all that nonsense – you can just download what you need and then print out some sort of certificate off the Internet, easy as that. And, in any case, if you apply for a job, no one ever checks on your qualifications anyway.

P.S. Just in case you're wondering, I did actually send my kids to school so that they could get into universities that I can't afford.

SELF-STORAGE UNITS

Apparently, Napoleon once described us as a nation of shopkeepers. Cheek! But that was probably only because his mistress used to spend all his money when she visited London on her regular shopping sprees. She would ask him if he wanted to join her on late-night opening, to which he famously replied, 'Not tonight, Josephine!'

Of course, that was hundreds of years ago when the rest of us were too poor to go shopping just for the sake of... shopping. The truth is that we were more than likely to be selling anything and everything but all we could really afford was to buy something to eat! Nowadays we're more likely to be described as a nation of shoppers, rather than shopkeepers.

Even if we're poor and don't have any spare cash, it doesn't seem to stop us spending every spare moment we have going out and buying stuff – stuff we don't really need. Buying for the sake of… buying! It's all so easy with the use of our 'flexible friends' (Of course, the credit and debit cards aren't our 'friends' at all – they are, in fact, our enemies) to spend, spend, spend on the Internet without even leaving our homes. It's all so convenient and our purchases are delivered to our very door. I equate it with an addiction like drugs, alcohol or trainspotting.

Now, I don't have a problem with going out shopping if you need something; something vital, such as the odd sausage or an inflatable – or even an inflatable sausage – but it's got to the stage where, even if your home is crammed full of objects or goods that you don't actually need, you continue to buy even more goods, until, eventually, you either have to move to a bigger house or build an extension just to make room for all the extra stuff you've been out and bought.

Naturally, it's more likely you can't afford to do either because you've already spent every spare penny you had and, in many cases, you're up to your eyeballs in debt so you opt for the next best thing… you rent a self-storage unit!

Up until a few years ago there wasn't such a thing – well, there was but it was for people who were between houses and needed to place their furniture somewhere. Another alternative, if you needed to make some room by getting rid of some possessions, was to head down to your local car-boot sale. The trouble was that you often ended up worse off because half the time you'd end up buying more items than you sold and most of it pretty ropey stuff, like mechanic's overalls, boxes of nail varnish, video cassettes (non-VHS) and fake brass rubbings.*

It appears we've become not only a nation of shoppers but a

nation of hoarders, and these storage units have simply added to the problem. Not only have we spent more money by buying stuff we don't actually need but we also have an extra monthly outgoing: the expense of renting a storage unit!

The answer is simple really, a bit like my diet plan: 'Don't buy bigger clothes.' So if you haven't got room for it, whatever it is, don't buy it. You don't bloody need it!

*Statistics provided by the Car-Boot Aficionados Association.

SHAGGY-DOG STORY

I love a good Shaggy-Dog Story – here's one of my favourites...

A butcher is busy when he notices a dog in the shop. He tries to shoo him away but the dog refuses to budge. He goes over to the dog and notices that there is a note in his mouth. The butcher takes the note, which reads, 'Can I have twelve sausages and a leg of lamb, please? The dog has money in its collar.' The butcher checks and, lo and behold, there is a twenty-pound note.

The butcher deposits the money and puts the sausages and lamb in a bag, placing it in the dog's mouth. The butcher is so impressed that he decides to close the shop and follow the dog. The dog walks down the street and approaches a pedestrian crossing. The dog puts down the bag, jumps up and presses the button. Then he waits patiently, bag in mouth, for the lights to turn. They do and he walks across the road, with the butcher following him all the way.

The dog then comes to a bus stop and checks the timetable. The butcher can't believe his eyes. The dog sits on the bench, picks up a copy of *The Times* and reads patiently. When the first bus arrives, the dog walks around to the front, looks at the number and goes back to his seat. Another bus comes. Again the dog goes and looks at the number and lets it go. The third bus arrives and, this time, he climbs on.

The butcher, by now open-mouthed, follows him onto the bus. The bus travels through the town and out into the suburbs, while the dog completes the crossword. Eventually, he gets up and moves to the front of the bus, where he stands on his two back legs and pushes the stop button.

Then he gets off, groceries still in his mouth. The dog, still closely followed by the butcher, walks along the road and then turns into a driveway. He walks up the path and drops the groceries on the step. Then he walks back down the path, takes a big run and throws himself with a huge bang against the door.

He goes back down the path, runs up to the door and throws himself against it again. There's no answer, so the dog goes back down the path, jumps up on a narrow wall and walks along the perimeter of the garden. He gets to the window and beats his head against it several times, walks back, jumps off and waits at the door.

The butcher watches as a man opens the door and starts swearing at the dog. The butcher runs up and stops the man. 'What on earth are you doing? The dog is a genius. He's brilliant. I've never known such a clever dog.'

The owner responds, 'Clever, my eye. This is the second time this week that he's forgotten his key.'

SHOE SHOPS

Another one of my pet hates is shopping for shoes, although I know that, for many women, it's an obsession. Marilyn Monroe once said, 'Give a girl the right shoes and she can conquer the world,' although I'm not sure many of her fans ever looked at her footwear!

Imelda Marcos, the widow of the former President of the Philippines, is probably best known for her collection of 3,000 pairs of shoes, of which nearly 800 are in a museum. I'm not a great one for museums at the best of times and, unless you are Jimmy Choo or have some sort of shoe fetish – or both – that's definitely one to avoid.

What I really hate about some shoe shops is the fact that it would appear the management doesn't trust you. So they hide half the bloody shoes. In most shops, even when you have found what you consider to be the perfect shoes, you have to take a number! It's a bit like going to A&E or a bakery. It's funny that both such places work on the same system of queuing. I once had to attend A&E when one of Derek's fins went into my eye and, because I couldn't see properly, I went into a bakery by mistake! I ended up with a crumpet instead of an eye patch and I can tell you the butter didn't help my eye at all.

Anyway, back at the shoe shop… You then have to wait until an assistant eventually calls out your number and he or she will then reluctantly disappear into the back stockroom, for what seems about half an hour, to search for the other shoe.

I can only assume they think you're going to run off with them, which is why they only let you have access to one shoe at a time. When you go out to buy a suit, both the jacket and trousers are there together on a hanger. You can pick up the whole 'whistle' (I bet you didn't know I am bilingual and speak fluent cockney) and take it into the changing room to try it on. They don't let you help yourself to the jacket but then take a number and wait because all the bloody trousers are hidden out the back!

Once, when trying on a pair of desert boots, I complained to the assistant that they were completely ill-fitting and that she must have given me the wrong size. She then pointed out that I had crossed my legs and I had put them on the wrong feet…

Unbelievable!!!

SMOKING

This may prove unpopular among some of you but then I'm not here not to upset some people. Sometimes I don't know why I'm here but it's certainly not to upset people. Every year we have a 'National No Smoking Day'. Well, I'm going to suggest a 'National Smoking Day'. There, I've said it. While you're taking in the enormity of that idea, let me explain…

Smokers save non-smokers a bloody fortune on TAX because some packets of cigarettes now cost almost £10 a packet – most of which is the tax. It costs far less to treat smokers' illnesses on the NHS than the government raise in tax on cigarettes so, if all the smokers gave up tomorrow, they'd have to raise taxes to cover the deficit. In fact, never mind a National Smoking Day, I'm now so agitated that, if it was up to me, we would have a 'NATIONAL EVERYONE SHOULD SMOKE DAY'!

SMOKING

Of course, in recent years the dreaded smoking ban has come into effect. What really annoys me is that it started in Europe and yet over there – while they may display a big 'No Smoking' sign on the outside of the premises – the actual counter area is often lined up with ashtrays. Half the people in there are sat smoking their heads off and no one seems to mind!

In this country it's a different story: no one dares defy the ban for fear of the 'smoking police' slapping an £80 fine on them – we're a compliant lot, us British! Having said that, in reality, when was the last time you actually heard of anybody being fined £80 for smoking inside? It hardly ever happens.

A few years ago I was attending a wedding (a great occasion: very enjoyable and romantic – obviously not one of my own!) The only trouble was that it was pouring with rain and so, not wanting to get wet, I stood inside the doorway puffing away. I thought, if I do get caught, it's only £20 more than a parking ticket and how often do we take a 'chance' for five minutes and pull up on yellow lines… anyway, I got away with it! To be honest, I've never actually seen any smoking police and am beginning to think they're a bit of a myth. But it does still make me cross.

I now need a fag to calm down and I can tell you it won't be one of those E-cigarettes. What are they all about? To me, it's not proper smoking. You won't see me with a personal vaporizer – sounds like something out of *Dr Who*! I can't imagine imbibing a liquid concoction and blowing out great plumes of smoke at passing strangers.

I wasn't even keen on those menthol-flavoured cigarettes.

To me, it's like inhaling a tube of Colgate toothpaste… and without 'The Ring of Confidence'. No, I was sad to see the back of the 'Wills Wild Gold Leaf Woodbine Super Tar'. And then, of course, there is the whole routine and paraphernalia of rolling your own, which I'm told, for some reason, was very popular in 1960s California. I know smoking isn't good for your health and has been described as a filthy habit but I can think of many other much filthier habits. (I won't list them, as this book is family friendly.)

There's much more I'd like to say but I might find myself in deep water, which can be even more dangerous to your health!

SPAIN

Ever since they invented the cheap package holiday, Spain has been a firm favourite with us Brits. The weather is, of course, a great draw – their winters are more like our summers – and it's also cheap. But for lots of Brits, donning their sombreros and dousing themselves in suntan lotion, holidaying on various Costas once or twice a year isn't enough. They actually take the plunge and leave good old Blighty to start a new life in the sun.

My sister Jenny and her husband Joe were two of those who decided to join the migration, bid farewell to the cold winters and fulfil their dream of running a bar in Spain. They headed to Fuengirola on the Costa del Sol.

Joe really hated the cold winters and was desperate to live all year round in a warm climate. It seemed a great idea. What could possibly go wrong? There was an added bonus in that he was a keyboard player – not the computer type but the one that plays a tune like on a piano. In fact, he was a professional musician and, in fairness, quite good, so they thought that, in order to make this particular bar popular and to bring the punters flocking, they would open it as a 'Piano Bar'. In addition, to ensure they could match their competitors, they also introduced a food menu.

So far, so good. Well… sort of…

The trouble was that, although Joe was good pianist, he had never run a bar and so, once he had the keys to his own place, he wasn't very sure what he was doing. Oh, and he didn't actually own a piano, just a small portable keyboard. Also my sister, bless her, hadn't worked much in a pub either, although she did spend a number of years working on the checkout in a supermarket, so she did know how to use a cash register! Jenny was certainly no chef – in fact, not even a great cook – but was more than capable of rustling up a good old fry-up or, indeed, anything with chips. She certainly wasn't going to serve up that Spanish 'pie-ella' stuff, although, to compete with those establishments that did, they had some pies on the menu.

Money was tight and they couldn't afford to employ any staff and so they had to do everything themselves. This wasn't a problem until someone actually ordered some food. Joe was busy 'belting' out the tunes and Jenny had to go into the kitchen to prepare the meal, which resulted in the fact that there was no one to serve the drinks at the bar.

So Joe and Jenny then introduced a self-service system, whereby the customers served themselves and put money in the till… I expect you can see where this is going…

Well, this system – I won't call it a plan – actually worked well for a while and, when word got out, they started to get quite busy. At first Joe and Jenny were delighted but then, surprisingly, the busier the bar became, the more money they seemed to lose! Perhaps it wasn't that surprising and my poor sister and her husband had become just too trusting and were being ripped off.

It wasn't long before they had no choice but to close the bar and, eventually, Jenny returned to England. Joe, however, hated the cold so much and was determined to remain in the nice warm sunshine to see out his days. So, despite his financial predicament, he decided to stay, working as a keyboard player in other people's bars.

My sister stayed in touch with him and a number of years later was very sad to receive a phone call to say that Joe had died the previous day. Jenny knew that they tend to have funerals very quickly in hot countries but she just couldn't get over immediately and so a few weeks later arranged a special service in her local church.

It was almost six months later when she finally made the visit to Spain to sort out the paperwork and get a copy of the death certificate (they were still officially married) and it was then that she discovered that, unlike most other things, funerals are expensive in Spain and, as he didn't have any money, he hadn't had one. Worse still, he hadn't been buried or cremated… he was still in the mortuary. Since his death, he'd been stuck in a freezer and, worse still, not only did Jenny then have to somehow raise the money for a cremation but they also billed her for keeping him in a freezer for six months.

It is, of course, a tragic story but there was something wonderfully ironic that Joe, who had stayed in Spain because he hated the cold, had ended up spending six months in a bloody deep freezer…

STAFF

Although I've enjoyed myself owning and managing hotels, the one element that has always been a pain in the neck is the staff! Difficult guests would come and go and usually not stay longer than a fortnight, but the staff were there every week!

While some were very good and loyal, some were hopeless and my biggest problem in the end was that I was almost too scared to sack anyone. Well… maybe not scared… it was just that I couldn't bloody afford to. I once got sued for unfair dismissal and was ordered to pay almost £20,000 to someone who I sacked because I thought they were bloody useless and were costing the business money. Well, it cost me alright! About TWENTY GRAND!!!

There was another time when a member of staff was suspected of stealing the chambermaids' tips by sneaking round the empty rooms on departure days. This really made me angry! Stealing from me was one thing, but the chambermaids had the hardest job in the entire hotel and, actually, earned the least money, so I felt this was particularly mean.

One of my managers set a trap. To verify the suspect's identity, he photocopied a five-pound note and then placed the fiver in one of the bedrooms. Sure enough, within twenty minutes the note had disappeared and, when we searched the suspect, we found it in her pocket. I sacked the thief on the spot!

Believe it or not, she took me to court and even more shockingly she won the case! I had to reinstate her because she claimed that someone else had been caught stealing from me in the past but hadn't actually been sacked for it. I had been lenient with them and so it was unfair to dismiss her for stealing. It was deemed 'unfair dismissal'. Unfair! Never mind unfair, it was unbelievable!

While sometimes I really miss the hotel business, other times I'm just grateful I don't have to put up with employing some of the staff I did. I can remember receiving a phone call from the chef at about 7.30 one morning. In a right panic, he told me that he and the rest of the kitchen staff had been stood outside waiting and couldn't get into the hotel to prepare the breakfast. They'd been banging on the door and ringing the bell for over half an hour! The hotel was full and, with over ninety breakfasts to cook, time was running out.

I employed a night porter, who was also the evening barman, and it was his job to look after the hotel at night. This wasn't one of those 'sleep-in jobs' – he was meant to be awake all night in case a guest had a problem, or for any emergencies. He also had a list of things he was expected to do, including tasks like tidying up, cleaning the lounge, etc.

I was just getting dressed and about to dash straight down to the hotel (I lived in a house about three miles away at the time) when the chef phoned me back. The panic was over. Some of the guests had heard all the commotion and banging and had come down and unbolted the front door to let the chef and the rest of the kitchen staff in. That was a relief, but where was the night porter?

Twenty minutes later I arrived at the hotel and noticed that the lounge hadn't been cleaned properly, the bar shutters were up and there was still no sign of the night porter. Then, as I peered over the bar, I saw something move. There, lying face down, snoring loudly, was the night porter with his trousers round his knees and still clutching an empty bottle of spirits. Not only was he drunk on duty but on my bloody whisky! My first reaction was to sack him there and then but then I thought, but what's the bloody point? He'd probably end up suing me for providing him with a cheap scotch, rather than a deluxe single malt.

The trouble is I'm a perfectionist and, having done all the staff jobs over the years, I know exactly how they should be done. If I had my way – and as I may have mentioned once or twice previously – I would have actually cloned myself to do every job in the entire hotel and I would only have employed myself!

T

TATTOOS

Tattooing has apparently been a custom since Neolithic times, which is apparently a very long time ago – even before Coronation Street was first screened – but now the 'art' seems to be making a huge comeback.

This is something I really don't understand, this latest craze to cover your body with tattoos. I know it's an old custom for sailors and servicemen and – don't get me wrong – some of them are really impressive, like mini works of art, but others are pretty ugly or pointless. I don't get the idea of having LOVE on one hand and HATE on the other, or branding your chest with the name of a girlfriend who's long dumped you or a wife who you've divorced – therefore making it embarrassing when you start dating or marrying again. (Well, it certainly wouldn't have been a good idea for me.)

Some people have MUM emblazoned on their arms. That's just daft. Now, don't get me wrong, I love my dear old mum, but I'm not about to have it tattooed anywhere. I also love Dunhill Cigarettes but I wouldn't dream of having the word DUNHILL tattooed across my buttocks, or anywhere else either for that matter.

It's surprising that, in recent years, tattoos have become even more popular with women. I blame these modern pop singers. They seem to be the ones who started it. I mean have you seen Lady Gaga? Unbelievable! She's got a whole book branded across her torso. I mean, you wouldn't have caught Doris Day with a picture of Cary Grant above her left breast, or the lovely Vera Lynn with a replica of the White Cliffs of Dover engraved across her back, would you?

What really concerns me is how these fabulous works of art are going to look when you are in your seventies. The flesh starts to sag and the skin goes all wrinkly. There's a reason why traditional works of art are put on canvas, which is then stretched and held into place by stapling it onto a wooden frame. You can't do that with a rib cage. Some of these women are going to get a shock as they get older!

It's also amusing when people have tattoos in Chinese, in which one wrong character can change the whole meaning of the message. One person, who thought they were bearing the slogan 'To find happiness', discovered their tattoo stated publicly, 'I am slow'! There are also some famous misspelled tattoos, such as: 'I am a ledgend', 'Only Gad can juge me', 'You are my sweet pee', 'No regerts', etc., etc. Tattastrophes, I think they call them. If they don't, they should do.

No, I have to be honest. I'm sorry but, despite how wonderful some of them may look, as far as I'm concerned, 'Tattoos are for sailors and gays!'

TELEVISION

John Logie Baird first invented the television in the 1920s (apparently, it wasn't Kanye West) and the premier broadcast was made in 1936 from the BBC studios in Alexandra Palace. It was quite an amazing achievement – the only trouble was that no one could watch it because he hadn't bothered to invent remotes. Apparently, it was only when Winston Churchill discovered one hidden under his sofa at Chequers during a bombing raid that the medium later became successful. What a man!

People are a bit snobbish about television and so some of the terms are a little derogatory. The 'idiot box' and the 'goggle box' are very unfair. And whenever I refer to the 'television set', any youngster in my hearing inevitably falls about.

To be honest (I've tried throughout the book to be as honest as my editor, lawyer and ex-wives will allow), I don't actually watch that much telly, although when I was a kid, I used to love watching things like *Morecambe and Wise*. And I had a special interest in them. You see, my father had, in fact, appeared with the legendary comedy duo at various music halls around the country many, many years ago when he was actually topping the bill, long before they became famous.

Years later, when they were really renowned, Eric and Ernie were appearing in Torquay and we went to see them. When they discovered that my dad was in the audience, they became really excited and were keen to see him after so many years. So, after the show, they invited us backstage to their dressing room to say hello. During this time, their television shows were getting twenty-five million viewers and they were, without doubt, this country's biggest stars. I was just nine years old and, as we entered the dressing room, I was in total awe. I was speechless (probably for the first and last time in my life)! I couldn't believe what I was seeing. And in real life too. Because there… yes… it was true… in the corner was… a 26-IN COLOUR TELEVISION SET! Not only had I never seen a TV that big before but the pictures were in colour! And here in the dressing room!

I swore there and then that, if I did go into show business, my ultimate dream would be to be famous enough to demand a 26-in colour TV in my dressing room!

I have to say that most things that are on TV get on my nerves. I can't bear some of those English soaps – why anyone watches *EastEnders* is beyond me. If I want to hear yelling and screaming and witness bad behaviour by coarse cockneys, I can just go to Nando's. And what about *Midsomer Murders*? You'd never know that the English countryside is actually a haven of peace and tranquillity when you're knee-deep in bloody corpses.

No, my fondest memories of television were of *Dallas* and the famous 'Bobby Ewing in the shower' scene. Bobby, played by Patrick Duffy, had been run down and killed by a car a year before but, in the next season of shows, he appeared to his wife, Pam, in the shower and casually bid her 'Good Morning!' It then dawned on her that his death was all a bad dream and that the previous thirty-one episodes hadn't actually happened! Ahh… the magic of television!

And then, of course, there's 'Reality TV', which, of course, I find fascinating – especially if I'm on! Ha! The first thing that people say to me when they meet me in 'real life' is usually, 'You look taller on the telly!' My reply is also a standard response: 'Ahh… but that depends how high your TV is off the ground!' People have often said to me that they'd love to see the 'outtakes' from *The Hotel* TV series… and I say, 'You did.' the programme was actually made up of the 'outtakes' and the things that went wrong!

Despite some of my reservations about the medium, I've got a lot to be grateful for when it comes to telly. You see… oh, wait a minute… I've just had a sudden thought… yes… it's a good job that electricity was also invented – otherwise we'd have to watch television in the dark. Think of that. Blimey!

TEXT TALK

I've never been one for foreign languages; I'm far too British for all that nonsense. I'm just grateful that the British Empire spread as far as it did to huge parts of the world, so that the most widely spoken language on this planet is, in fact, ours: English.

I know far more people actually speak Chinese but that's only because there are so many of them – and most of them live in China, so it doesn't really count!

When I was at school, they did try and teach me a few French words but I wasn't really interested. I tried to explain that Spanish would have been more useful. I mean, who goes on holiday to France anyway? Spain, yes, but not France! I wouldn't mind but the French don't even like us, so why bother learning their language?

When I do go abroad to non-English speaking countries, I have a basic rule, which I apply if I need to buy something: if the shopkeeper or waiter can't be bothered to learn to speak my language, they obviously don't want my money and so I find another shop or restaurant that does. (Having said that, I have always found that repeating myself and speaking slower and louder seems to help…)

But, in recent years, it seems we have been invaded with a whole new language – no, not that Esperanto nonsense! I mean, what sort of a daft idea is that? The Polish chap who invented it had obviously not travelled much because, if he had got around a bit more, he'd have realised there was already an international language: English!

No, I'm talking about the dreaded 'text talk'. For ages I

genuinely thought 'LOL' simply meant 'Lots Of Love'. Then I was informed it actually means 'Laugh Out Loud' but, apparently, it *could* sometimes mean 'Lots Of Love' (you have to just know which one is meant – otherwise you can get into a pickle). Gr8!!! (That's 'Great', BTW). 'BTW' is 'By The Way', which is no help if you're texting your sweetheart sweet nothings and you have no idea whether you're being laughed at or not.

The alternative to 'LOL' is 'ROTFL' (Roll On The Floor Laughing) – although, of course, I've never heard anyone actually say that in real life! And when was the last time you actually said 'LMAO' (Laugh My Ass Off) or 'IMHO' (In My Humble Opinion)?

I 'H8' (Hate) text talk… I think the killer is that they even have this one: 'WLUMRyME?', which means 'Will You Marry Me?' Can you imagine getting a marriage proposal by text? Not exactly Romeo and Juliet, is it? My answer would be, 'NUYLTSPE' (Not Until You Learn To Speak Proper English).

Unbelievable!!! 'TTFN' (Ta-Ta For Now).

TOMATOES

Apparently, tomatoes are a fruit – I've even looked it up and it says so on the Internet. For your information, it's the berry of the nightshade *Solanum lycoperscium* – I didn't have to look that up, actually, as I already knew that bit, having run a 'Latin for Beginners' evening at one of my hotels. Not one of my most successful events, although the man who came in a Salsa dress seemed to quite enjoy himself. But that's another story… Anyway, if the tomato is a fruit, when was the last time you ordered a fruit salad and found a tomato in it? If tomatoes really are a fruit, you'd think that's the one place you'd find them.

For years people avoided eating tomatoes because they thought they belonged to the 'Deadly Nightshade' family – a lethal poison. And, as I think of tomatoes as a vegetable, I still consider them poisonous and keep a safe distance. I can quite understand why crowds used to pelt actors at live performances during Elizabethan times with rotten tomatoes. Best thing to do with them. I'm glad to say I've never had anything thrown at me during one of my Party Nights, although a woman once threatened me with an inflatable radish.

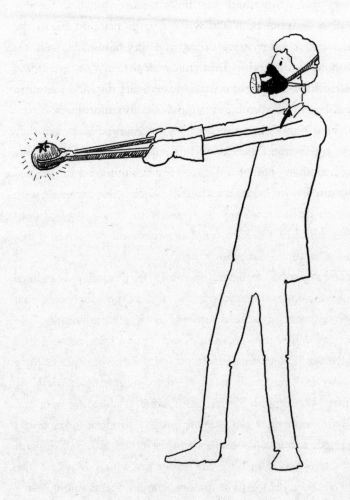

TORQUAY

There was a time, back in the Victorian era, when Torquay used to be quite posh and was quite the place to be. In the nineteenth century it was considered very fashionable and was favoured by the crème de la crème of Victorian society. It was even compared with the sophisticated, elegant Mediterranean coastal town of Montpelier – unfavourably, unfortunately.

Those rich Victorian types built huge, grand villas like they were going out of fashion, which, of course, they were. Nowadays, most of them have been extended beyond recognition and what used to be a delightful four-bedroom villa, complete with servants quarters, is now more likely to be a forty-bedroom hotel, a bit like The Grosvenor or, worse still, converted into a load of cramped and gloomy flats.

The resort had its heyday in the 1970s, just before the cheap package holiday became popular and people discovered that Spain enjoyed guaranteed sunshine. Don't get me wrong: I love Torquay. When the sun shines on the palm trees and glorious sandy beach, it is, without doubt, one of the best places for a holiday and you really don't need to go abroad. It is rightly named 'The English Riviera'. But, when it's pouring with rain and you're sat in a café staring out the window, looking at a deserted, windswept beach, it's not so much fun and difficult to pretend you're in Nice, St-Tropez or Cannes. Maybe a film festival at the Princess Theatre or Central Cinema might help – I could help cut the ribbon.

Worse still is losing all your money in one of the many amusement arcades, which doesn't make for the best of holidays. I've never had much luck in those places, although I did once apply for a job at an arcade. I didn't get it because in the interview I admitted I was scared of change.

Still, there's always the 'Agatha Christie Mile', which is a walking tour (with plaques) you can take and which is dedicated to the life and work of the great 'whodunnit' author. I've always wanted to take it but never found out 'whodoesit'.

I've lived the majority of my life in Sunny Torquay and over the years I have left a few times but each time I've somehow been drawn back and noticed the changes. I can remember when Torquay had a Rolls-Royce dealership and, when I moved back, I noticed it had changed and had become a Skoda garage. That just shows you…

Since appearing in *The Hotel*, it would appear I've become a bit of a 'Marmite' character in Torquay. Luckily, most people are very friendly and happy about the TV show and seem to like me, but the tourist board didn't care for the programme, claiming the way that Torquay was portrayed didn't help the town at all. They said I'd set them back twenty to thirty years! Well, I had my answer. I told them, 'You should be bloody grateful because Torquay was a much better place twenty to thirty years ago and much more popular than it is today!'

Maybe the real problem was that the tourist board didn't really like the Dolphin Racing (see 'I' for INFLATABLES) that I introduced to Torquay and with which Torquay is now associated.

So, on that basis, I can only assume that not only are they a miserable lot but they're not dolphin friendly!

𝓤

UFOs

Are there such things as UFOs? Well, according to some, the answer is definitely 100 per cent yes, although quite why these superior intelligent beings would bother to travel billions of light years through space just to find some crazy half-wits and transport them aboard their space craft in order to stick probes up their bottom, I just don't know. I can only assume that these super-intelligent aliens think that's where the abductees' brains are located! The fact that they then immediately head back home just as mysteriously as they have appeared without bothering to make their presence known to any of the normal, sane, rational humans on this planet has also always baffled me!

Anyway… back to the original question: are there such things as UFOs? Well, I suppose the answer, in a way, is sort of 'yes' because, if the person seeing the object could recognise them, they'd actually be Identified Flying Objects!

During the late 1940s and through the 1950s, UFOs were often referred to as 'Flying Saucers' when there was a fear – particularly in America – of alien invasions. There were loads of sightings and even photographs of supposed spacecraft in various forms. Of course, it has since been established that most UFO observations turn out to be normal everyday objects or natural phenomena, such as aeroplanes, hot air balloons, strangely formed clouds, meteors or astronomical objects, such as bright planets. I suppose a bright planet couldn't be termed as an 'everyday object' but you know what I mean!

There were a number of hoaxes whereby people pretended they'd seen a UFO and 'proved' it with scientific evidence, such as a close-up snap of a saucepan lid suspended from a tree (it was always the string that always gave it away), actual saucers that turned out to be plastic, or someone holding an aluminium cigar tube in the air. Some fraudsters even claimed to have discovered the bodies of aliens in fields – which invariably turned out to be origami or made of plasticine or Lego.

Alien abductions and Martian invasions were all the rage at one stage. Alien abductions, I ask you! What a load of rubbish – unless, of course, the *Men in Black* films are true to life and we're actually surrounded with aliens who are posing as humans. What nonsense. Absolute claptrap. Although, having said that, it wouldn't surprise me to learn that Katie Hopkins is actually from another planet. By the way, did you know that the reason E.T. was so wide-eyed was that he'd just seen the phone bill!!

I'm quite sceptical about a lot of these instances and something of a conspiracy theorist:

THE KENNEDY ASSASSINATION – I think he's actually still alive (I saw a dead ringer of JFK in Nether Wallop the other day),

CROP CIRCLES (caused by sozzled farmers on wayward tractors) and, most of all, THE MOON LANDINGS. I'm one of those that isn't really convinced that man has actually landed on the moon. I still think it was the Americans showing off and trying to convince Russia that they were cleverer than them. No, as far as I'm concerned, the whole 'landing' was staged on a Hollywood sound stage with help from the Disney Corporation and using defunct cameras and a dodgy sound system. I agree with The Flat Earth Society that the Apollo Astronauts were filmed on a fake moon landscape, as there is 'incorrect shadow and lack of background stars'. Another theory is that the backdrop to the moon looks uncannily like some green belt in Milton Keynes (some people claim they can see a concrete cow in the background – and it's not the one that jumped over the moon). In any case, there's a distinct lack of atmosphere in all footage.

Of course, if we are ever visited by beings from another planet and we do find it's been true all along and they land on earth, these objects will no longer be 'Unidentified'.

They'll become just plain old FOs!!!

UMBRELLLAS

For most people, umbrellas are useful gadgets for staying dry when it's raining cats and dogs, which is generally considered the worst sort of weather, except in Manchester when that kind of a day is considered 'a bit of a scorcher'. Personally, I'm not a great fan of umbrellas − I think they are, at best, dangerous weapons or, at worst, implements of torture (or should that be the other way round?).

Actually, it's more to do with the people who carry them: 'Clever Dicks' who think they are better prepared than you and me (unless, of course, Dear Reader, you are that 'Clever Dick' type) and who brandish them with a false pride and a look of self-satisfaction and haughtiness. In fact, to my mind, there isn't anything more smug than the bearer of an umbrella.

Anxiously peering up into the stratosphere, they can't wait for the first raindrop, when they can triumphantly burst open their rain protector and look at the rest of us fair-weather types with disdain and pity. And that's when the trouble can start, for they have no regard for any health-and-safety etiquette! They wield their umbrellas with total abandon and are more than likely to take your eye out. Unbelievable!

Then, of course, you get couples walking side by side and blocking the entire pavement so that you have to squeeze past them and hope that you are not trapped between the two brollies. They never think of raising them above their heads so that you can get by. (In my case, they only need to lift them up above their waists to allow me safe passage.) Umbrellas are also useless in stormy weather, when the material gets blown inside out and you have a hideous skeleton, which serves no purpose at all! You see them abandoned all over the streets and have to be careful when you step over them not to get a spike through your foot.

Personally, I think it's more macho to get wet and catch man flu, take to your bed and moan about being ill for weeks on end than utilise the services of an umbrella, although I have to admit that I have, on the rare occasion, used one. The trouble is I'm not very adept with the workings and, inevitably, I end up entangled with an oncoming umbrella enthusiast. Naturally, it's never someone who you might want to become entangled with. I mean, it's never a gorgeous model like Kate Moss or even someone who looks like Kylie Minogue – more than likely, it's some bully-boy type who uses their umbrella as a threatening cudgel and will hook the handle around your ankles and bring you crashing to the ground if he doesn't like the cut of your jib.

And, of course, there's always someone in a rainstorm who, to impress their girlfriend or grandmother, has to attempt a Gene Kelly impersonation in a rendition of 'Singing in the Rain'. It's always inevitable that they can neither sing nor dance and probably don't even bother to wear galoshes.

Please don't get me started on parasols and sunshades – they are all in the same category, as far as I'm concerned. The word 'umbrella' is actually derived from the Latin word 'umbra', meaning shade. I mean, what's the point in going to a beach and skulking in the shade? You go to a beach for one reason and one reason only and that's to lie out in the sun, turn pink and spend the whole holiday in agony from sunburn. It's traditional and simply British.

I suppose a bit like the umbrella.

USA

When Barack Obama was first elected, they made a big deal about having a black president and it was, indeed, of great historical significance. But I'd be even more impressed if the president of the USA was a Red Indian. All right, all those smoke signals wouldn't be good for global warming but he could solve so many of the world's problems by offering all his enemies a peace pipe and, if that didn't work, the threat of being scalped would definitely be effective.

They say that you call someone who speaks two languages 'bilingual' but you call someone who speaks one language 'American'! You see, that's another thing about the USA that I don't understand – their whole spelling thing. I mean, Americans speak English. They don't claim to speak 'American' and readily accept that they don't have a language of their own. Not many of them now speak 'Native American' or 'Red Indian' and those that did had the right idea of accusing the incoming settlers of talking with 'a forked tongue'. I think that may have been something to do with stealing all their land and forcing them onto reservations – but I'm sure the misuse of English also came into play.

So, if Americans speak English, how come some of the spellings are so wrong? When the first dictionaries arrived, there must have been some pages missing or they must have been devised by someone who couldn't spell properly. For instance, 'jelly' became 'jello'. That really is incomprehensible. It seems that everything has to be done quicker in the USA and so some of their spellings are really lazy: I mean, when did 'night' suddenly become 'nite'?

And it's not just the spelling – there are some daft words and expressions that make no sense at all. 'Homely' in American means ugly. Well, that can get you into all sorts of trouble when you visit someone's house across the pond. 'Pants' are trousers, which can get you into even more trouble. I once overheard someone say, 'She's dumb – she never stops talking.' It's all very confusing. And they seem to have a big problem in America with anything French: when did chips become 'French fries'? And what about 'French toast'? What's that all about? That isn't French at all. The French would never do such a thing with bread, milk and an egg, although they do some very strange things with frogs' legs and snails. Equally bizarre is that Americans use the term 'faucet' instead of 'tap'. If you're in a restaurant, they don't say, 'Would you like bottled or faucet water?' The waiter offers you 'bottled or tap water', so, if they know that water comes out a tap, why don't they just say it?

I'm not even going to mention that in America your bum is actually called your 'fanny'. And next time I'm in New York on holiday and run out of cigarettes, I'll make sure I don't go up to the nearest passer-by and say, 'I'm looking for a fag.'

No, the Americans are a bit clueless when it comes to the proper use of English. Some of them are a bit dim – or, I should say, there are a lot of 'meatheads' in the USA!

P.S. Dear Editor, if we do sell this book to the USA, I suggest we remove this section altogether and replace with the US Constitution – not only will we increase sales and endear ourselves to the ever over-patriotic Americans but we could probably double the size of the book for very little work.

V

VANITY

There is, of course, nothing wrong with having pride in your appearance. I am of the opinion that you should always make the best of yourself and try to look as attractive as possible – as long as you don't step into conceit, which can lead you onto the path of narcissism and then onto the motorway of egotism. (I knew one man who was so conceited that he joined the navy so that the world could see him.)

Anyway, there was a time when the idea of vanity was reserved just for the fairer sex but times have certainly changed. In days gone by, apart from some sort of shaving cream (unless you were too lazy to shave, so you just grew a beard instead), the only product you were ever likely to find in a man's bathroom cabinet was a bar of soap… and that's if you were lucky!

Back in those days the most exotic thing used by men that really bothered about their appearance would have been a pot of Brylcreem hair gel, which first appeared in 1928 – coincidentally, the same year as Bruce Forsyth, who is now a stranger to hair gel!

But nowadays it's all completely different. Today's modern man is expected to go through almost the same daily palaver as women do and a huge range of products have been created aimed specifically at men. Chemists and stores are full of the stuff, such as: face and body washes; grooming creams for the day, night and all times in between; pre- and post-shave gels; eye-care solutions; and moisturisers. There is also 'extract-of-lemon lip balm', 'strawberry tanning mousse' and 'essence-of-lime shave cream'. Honestly, if you used all those, you'd end up smelling like a fruit salad.

There are, inevitably, many more different types of aftershaves and anti-perspiration sprays than you can shake a deodorant stick at. The choice is unbelievable and, whenever I do go shopping for such items, I end up standing in the appropriate aisle in Boots having no idea what I should choose. I mean, what sort of odour do I want to emit? If the idea is to pass on a scent that will attract a woman, how do you know what the opposite sex wants you to smell like? I mean, these women seem to love their perfumes so maybe the way to attract one is to wear a woman's scent!

The adverts are of no help. I wouldn't mind but most of them are complete nonsense and very misleading. I once tried some of that Lynx deodorant stuff. Did any women jump on me and start ripping my clothes off while I was sat outside Starbucks having a coffee and a fag? No, not a single one. In fact, hundreds of women walked by without even noticing my existence. So no change there. I can actually create that reaction without splashing out on a special deodorant.

Last Christmas I received a gift set containing lots of different men's products – I had no idea what half of them were actually for. And, believe it or not, there was a moisturiser made by a company called Bulldog! Why would anyone want to look like a bulldog? That has to be the least appealing name for a range of men's beauty products. I mean, who in their right mind wants to look like Alan Sugar?

Sorry but these products are just not for me. No, if I need to be groomed, healed or energised, there's only one answer. The solution isn't found in a bottle. Beauty and contentment comes from within… within a cup of coffee and packet of cigarettes!

VEGETARIANS

I really don't understand this whole vegetarian thing. When I was younger, vegetarianism hadn't even been invented... there was no such thing as a vegetarian. It's one of these modern fads, like health food. Someone recently told me about a new diet: a combination of yeast and shoe polish. Apparently, it's for people who like to rise and shine.

I mean, I can sort of understand that some people don't want to eat animals – I don't really like the thought of eating animals either and I'm a carnivore. In fact, I only eat meat and don't eat any vegetables at all! I won't eat anything green – especially cheese that has gone off.

But what I don't understand is why, if you don't want to eat meat because it comes from animals, you would want your food to look like it comes from something that you don't want to eat. I don't ask the butcher to dye my sausages orange so they look like carrots! I don't want to eat carrots!!

You see, nowadays they sell everything that isn't as it appears. The list is endless: vegetarian sausages, bacon, ham, burgers, mince, turkey. Even bloody vegetarian haggis. Now, I ask you, why would a vegetarian want to pretend they are eating a sheep's insides?!? The thing about haggis is that it looks like a football but you don't kick it, you eat it. But when you've eaten it, you wished you had kicked it. You know, I didn't realise that they even had vegetarians in Scotland. I suppose there must be some; perhaps they should just stick to deep-fried Mars bars and other such delicacies.

Now vegans are a different breed (luckily, they also start with 'v', otherwise I'd have to have a cross-reference, which could be a headache for my editor who, by the way, is a lovely girl and a good honest carnivore…). Anyway, as I was saying before I so rudely interrupted myself, vegans are very pure – they won't even use soap. Mind you, I've come across a lot of people in the hotel trade who don't use soap and they weren't vegans! And have you ever tried some of the meat substitutes? Tofu is made by coagulating soy milk and then pressing it into white squares. They say it's versatile – well, so is bubble wrap, and probably more tasty.

And one thing I've always wondered about vegetarians: if they go to bed and can't sleep, do they start counting nut cutlets?

VOL-AU-VENTS

There was a time when I thought canapés were what you used to cover guests at weddings but, after many years in hotel management, I'm much wiser about them now. And, as far as I'm concerned, the vol-au-vent is the king of the canapé, although, in these times of 'Equal Opportunities', maybe I should refer to it as the princess. Someone once described a vol-au-vent as some puff pastry with some meat stuffed inside it but this is to do the noble titbit a great disservice. To my mind, no party is complete without the vol-au-vent, which translates from the French as 'windblown'. (Please insert your own joke here. That's not because it's obvious – I just couldn't think of one.)

VOL-AU-VENTS

As in many other things, size does matter. Personally, I favour the small, bite-size vol-au-vent, which is easy to devour in two gulps and causes very little mess (known as a *bouchée* in some circles outside Torquay), but others prefer a larger morsel that may even require a two-handed approach. It's surprising how much controversy this can cause. In Budleigh Salterton I once witnessed two canapé enthusiasts come to blows over the parameters of a particular vol-au-vent.

There are, of course, various fillings you can use: chicken and mushroom, salmon and cucumber, Stilton and spinach (yuck) are popular but, to my mind, nothing is as mouth-watering as the chipolata and gravy filling. (Scrumptious – although I always need to take a shower afterwards.)

Although I'm running the risk of this tome becoming a recipe book (hey, that's not a bad idea for my next book. Editor, please take note!), I must mention that other sorts of hors d'oeuvres and finger food are also available. My other top tip for party food is cheese★ and pineapple on sticks… except don't use sticks – not only are they a health-and-safety hazard but they add to the clearing up. Instead of sticks, put your cheese and pineapple and cocktail sausages on Twiglets. They are much less messy and they taste delicious!

★You may have to use a special cheese, although that does increase the expense.
(Apologies about all the brackets in this section but I thought it clever.)
(Like the casing around a vol-au-vent.)

W

I've always thought 'W' to be a funny letter, especially as it's called a 'double U'... the way it's formed it looks more like it should be called 'double V' and it wouldn't make any difference to how we use it because the sound isn't used anyway!

(Sorry to interrupt your reading: I just thought I'd point that out. Now where was I? Oh yes... 'W'.)

WALES

You Welsh folk don't like having to pay to get back into your own country. I mean, look at the toll on the Severn Bridge in Bristol – they charge you to go into Wales but let you out for free. So Wales must actually be quite a nice place for so many people to stay there when they could escape!

I've always admired the Welsh (although I'm not that

keen on their national emblem – the leek. I do like daffodils, though.) They must be very clever because to pronounce all those difficult words is hard enough in English but, amazingly, they do it in Welsh. Now, that's what I call impressive. Well done, you lot!

Some people think I'm Welsh because I'm called Jenkins but I'm not. Well, that's not quite true because, when I say I'm not Welsh, I am... well, I may have a Welsh background but I'm not actually called Jenkins. And when I say I'm not called Jenkins, I am. But my grandfather wasn't. Well, he was actually but, you see, he wasn't called Jenkins when he was born. According to family legend, he changed his name to escape the rest of the family and fled to Canada. Apparently, his grandfather was a duke and he was a baron... and someone was trying to kill someone... and a coffin was buried full of stones and... that's another book entirely.

WINE

The whole idea of keeping a wine cellar has always been a complete mystery to me. I just don't comprehend that the more the wine goes out of date, the more expensive it becomes! I don't mind grape juice – it's actually quite nice and a lovely deep-purple colour. But wine is another story. Why anyone would want to drink it, let alone pay a fortune for a really old bottle, is beyond me.

And let's face it, to my mind, wine is actually grape juice that has gone off. It's been left hanging around for so long that, eventually, it ferments and isn't fit to drink anymore, which is why, when you do drink it, you start to get confused and the more you drink, the more confused you get till, eventually, you have no idea what you're doing and half the time you end up throwing up...

And it doesn't end there because the following day you wake up feeling like crap... but it's your own fault! If it's out of date, don't drink it. You wouldn't willingly buy other drinks and food that are beyond their sell by date and which could make you ill, so why do it with WINE? I think that a lot of the appeal is to do with snobbery.

Look at the nonsense about drinking port, which is just fortified wine and probably even more poisonous. Passing it to the left at dinner parties and all that rubbish. And did you know that, if someone forgets to pass on the decanter, it is very bad manners to ask for it directly? Instead, you have to ask the person who is hogging it, 'Do you know the Bishop of Norwich?' It is then presumed the guilty party will realise their terrible mistake and pass along the decanter – after apologising, of course.

That's why I like grape juice – there are no such snooty traditions and you don't have to pretend to know a bishop or even a vicar. You certainly don't have to own a decanter. You can drink grape juice from a cardboard box and, I promise you, no one will complain if you pass them the carton anti-clockwise.

WORK

While many consider it a four-letter word, for me, it's always been what I do and, generally, I'm quite good at it... Well, when

I say 'good at it', I always give everything I do 110 per cent, even if the result isn't what I hoped for. I've always believed it's better to try and fail than not try at all. To me, failing is when you don't try!

I've never actually had any proper hobbies or interests – apart from smoking and drinking coffee, although I'm not sure if they count as pastimes! I do like nice cars (especially Bentleys!), which I see as my reward for working hard, but, without other distractions, work is my life.

I actually started busking on the streets when I was just four years old (you'll be able to read more about that in my autobiography – but not for a while as I haven't written it yet!) and then progressed to entertaining in my parents' hotel (my dad always wanted me to be a professional entertainer).

My first job was when I was twelve years old and I got an evening paper round delivering the local newspaper. If I'm honest, that didn't go well because where we lived at the time was really hilly – far too hilly to try and ride a bike – so I had to do my round on Shanks' pony.

My first day was a bloody nightmare... I started on a Thursday and the paper sack was so heavy (I think it was car and property advertising day) I could hardly lift it. As I set off from the newsagent, it started to rain and it was already beginning to get dark.

It wasn't long before I became lost (it was PSN then – Pre-SatNav) and, although the paper shop wasn't that far from where I lived, the streets that I had to deliver to were roads I'd never been to before. In the dark, in terrible weather and half blinded by the rain on my glasses, I had no idea where I was going. I couldn't see a bloody thing!

I started to panic and never mind delivering the bloody papers, I couldn't find my way back to the paper shop and, even worse, I couldn't find my way home! I had visions of being stuck out all night in the cold and wet and I became really scared, to the point where I started to cry. Just then I saw a light at the end of the road… was it…? Yes, it was! It was shining and red and welcoming and brought joy to my heart. It was a telephone box – a TELEPHONE BOX! (For younger readers, mobiles hadn't been invented back then either.) I reached into my pocket but found… NOTHING – not even a 2-p piece! Well, of course, I didn't have any money. That's why I'd taken the bloody job in the first place!

Fortunately, I remembered that you could ask the operator to reverse the charges, which is exactly what I did, and it wasn't long before my dad was on the phone.

'Where are you?' he asked.

'In a phone box,' I replied, still sobbing.

Dad reassured me: 'Stay where you are and I'll come and find you!'

About thirty minutes later, having driven up and down every road in the area, my dad appeared. I'd never been so delighted to see him. 'Come on. Let's get you home,' he said.

'No… I can't,' I said, still tearful. 'I've still got all these papers to deliver.'

So good old Dad drove me to each and every house on the list until all the papers had been delivered – albeit a bit later than planned. Hooray! I gave my notice in the following day but finished the week's work and managed not to get lost again.

A couple of months later, in the summer holidays, I got a real job working in a café, operating the dishwashing machine and it wasn't long before – at the tender age of twelve – I was clocking up sixty hours a week, and have never really stopped since. I've set up and run a string of businesses since then, including a painting-and-decorating company called Van Gogh and a fish-and-chip shop in Blackpool, famed for its twice-battered, 18-in 'Monster Fish'.

I have, of course, considered other jobs: I considered becoming a physiotherapist but, although I'm used to hard graft, I really didn't fancy working my fingers to the bone. If I was going to work in a hospital, I'd have been better off being a dietician – that way I could have lived off the fat of the land!

But I couldn't imagine any other job than what I do now. I love entertaining people and seeing them enjoying themselves. What a lovely way to live and work!

XYLOPHONE

Could someone please explain why xylophone starts with an 'x'? It just doesn't make sense. It should start with a 'z'. I wouldn't mind, but the word doesn't even have a 'z' in it. Xylophone has to be the daftest spelling of a word in the entire English language and yet it's used to educate children when they first learn the alphabet. No wonder children are confused. I mean, that's about the worst example you can get for the use of the letter 'x'! And what about words that sound like they should begin with an 'x', like 'expectation', 'express' or 'excite', which actually start with an 'e'? It's bloody illogical.

Why don't the authorities just be honest and 'xplain' (see what I did there?) that no proper words – well, none that you would ever use unless you're some kind of scrabble champion

– actually begin with an 'x', apart, of course, from the TV show *X Factor*!

If it was up to me, we'd simplify the entire English language. We could go through the complete dictionary, correcting all the misspelled words, especially those ridiculous silent letters, which we could get rid of and then spell everything as it sounds. It would make life much easier for children and adults and, of course, for foreigners coming here. I think it would be a bit like when decimal coins came in – we set a date and, for a while, put both spellings in till everyone gets used to it. Quite simple really. Sometimes I surprise myself with my genius and (K)NOWLEDGE!!!

P.S. I would just to like to add, however, that I'd keep the 's' in The Grosvenor Hotel but move it to where it should be: GroveSnor!

Y

YORKSHIRE PUDDINGS

Despite my strange eating habits and lack of interest in food generally, Sunday lunch has always been a special time for me and something to look forward to — not just because, when the children were younger, it was often the only meal that we would all share together as a family.

As we are now on to the letter 'y', you will have gleaned that I only eat meat without vegetables and certainly nothing green. I had to add some other delicacy to my Sunday roast, apart from the gravy, of course. Yes, you've guessed it: the wonderful Yorkshire pudding! And, of course, it is so delicious that we didn't just keep that pleasure for when we had roast beef like you were supposed to: on Sundays it was Yorkshires with everything. Hooray!

In fact, to fill up my plate so it didn't look quite as lonely as it usually did, I'd often have four or even five of them. Now, these were proper Yorkshire puddings. Homemade too! Well, when I say 'homemade', they obviously came out of a packet. But there was some cooking involved, as you still had to mix in the egg and water and, naturally, half the fun was wondering whether the batter would rise or not.

The secret was all in the amount of oil in the baking tray and the temperature – the hotter the better! You also had to get the mixture just right and it didn't always go to plan. To be honest, my wife wasn't the best of cooks and sometimes they'd turn out like mini pancakes. Other times they'd stick to the tin tray and, by the time you scraped them out, what you could get onto your plate resembled some sort of scrambled egg. But no matter: we were never deterred from our weekly tradition because we always had next Sunday to look forward to!

The trouble is that things have now changed and I blame 'Aunt Bessie'. What was once a weekly treat has become an anytime, any-day option with the introduction of the frozen Yorkshire pud. There is no more guesswork or tense trial-and-error experiments – it's out of the freezer and into the oven. Three minutes later they're done. Of course, these frozen replicas of 'real' Yorkshire puddings taste a bit 'rubbery' to me, but it doesn't seem to put people off. In fact, 'Aunt Bessie' (does anyone know her real identity? I reckon it might be Gordon Ramsay in disguise) has actually gone a step too far and introduced those giant ones. Apparently, the idea is that, once you've put them on your plate, you can fill them with huge portions of food and your whole dinner is surrounded by pud. Must be a Northern thing…

I must admit, however, a few weeks ago, when my oven broke, I was grateful to 'Aunt Bessie' (or Gordon). I was so desperate not to miss out on my beloved Sunday dinner that I devised a cunning plan: I went out and bought some cooked slices of beef and a packet of Aunt Bessie's frozen Yorkshires and, while the microwave was heating up the meat and the kettle boiled to make the gravy, I flattened out the frozen Yorkshires and popped them in the toaster. Brilliant! Worked beautifully. Next stop, *MASTERCHEF*!!!

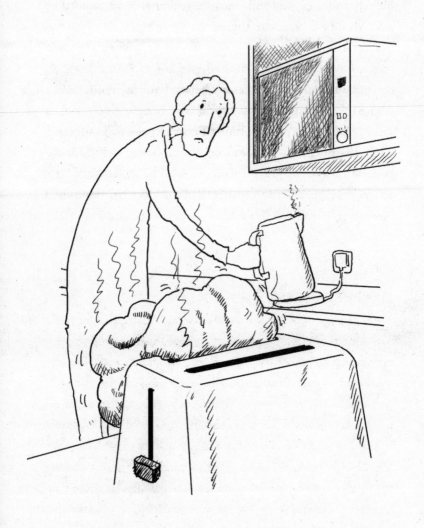

Z

ZOROASTRIANISM

Now, I know I could have found another word and a far easier topic for the letter 'z', which is one of those letters wrongly pronounced by those lazy Americans, who tend to take the easy route and, as such, have taken the '-ed' sound off the end of 'z' and replaced it with two or maybe more 'e's, so that zebra no longer sounds like 'zedbra' and is pronounced 'zeebra' instead. But I thought I'd like to finish this book on a high and prove once and for all to those doubters that I am, in fact, far cleverer than I look and that this book is certainly worth far more than the paper it's printed on. I think you might agree with me that this A–Z is, actually, a true hive of knowledge, a huge font of wisdom and a gigantic lexicon of insight – as well as a treasure trove of clichés.

THE WORLD ACCORDING TO MANAGER MARK

Zoroastrians, as they're commonly known, are followers of an ancient religion known as Zoroastrianism. Zoroastrianism is, in fact, an 'ancient semi-dualistic monotheist religion of Greater Iran', whatever that means! And so what really impresses me is that all that time ago, in ancient times, the spelling capabilities and range of vocabulary of the earth-dwellers was obviously far superior than it is today. It must have been if they were able to use words like Zoroastrianism and actually knew not just what they meant but how to spell them – and all without the benefit of Google or even the *Oxford English Dictionary*!

So I suggest, in order to impress your friends at dinner parties, book groups or Party Nights, you make a note of the definition of Zoroastrianism and carry it with you at all times. And there's always the chance that one day you might find yourself in a surprise game of Scrabble in which you spot the word 'Trains' on the board with at least a seven-letter gap in front of it and you have the letters Z O R O A S as your final ones. Your opponent probably won't know how to spell Zoroastrians and you'll amass hundreds of points, especially if the 'z' is on a triple-letter score or, better still, if the lot gets you onto a triple-word score. You'd become the toast of the Scrabble world and probably end up in *The Guinness Book of Records* and this would all be THANKS TO ME!

Well, that's it – that's the end. I've run out of letters. If you've enjoyed this book, please tell everyone and if you didn't... then just keep quiet. But I bet you didn't think you'd learn so much from reading this book, did you?

I reckon I could be in for the Booker Prize.

Blimey! That really would be unbelievable. HOORAY!!!